AF748839

Online Misogyny as a Hate Crime

The ideal of an inclusive and participatory Internet has been undermined by the rise of misogynistic abuse on social media platforms. However, limited progress has been made at national – and to an extent European – levels in addressing this issue. In England & Wales, the tackling of underlying causes of online abuse has been overlooked because the law focuses on punishment rather than measures to prevent such abuses. Furthermore, online abuse has a significant impact on its victims that is underestimated by policymakers. This volume critically analyses the legal provisions that are currently deployed to tackle forms of online misogyny and focuses on three aspects; first, the phenomenon of social media abuse; second, the poor and disparate legal responses to social media abuses; and third, similar failings of the hate crime provisions to tackle problems of online gender-based abuses. This book advances a compelling argument for legal changes to the existing hate crime, and communications legislation.

Kim Barker is Lecturer in Law at Stirling University.

Olga Jurasz is Senior Lecturer in Law at The Open University.

Online Misogyny as a Hate Crime

A Challenge for Legal Regulation?

Kim Barker and Olga Jurasz

Routledge
Taylor & Francis Group
LONDON AND NEW YORK

An electronic version of this book is freely available, thanks to the support of libraries working with Knowledge Unlatched (KU). KU is a collaborative initiative designed to make high quality books Open Access for the public good. The Open Access ISBN for this book is 9780429956805. More information about the initiative and links to the Open Access version can be found at www.knowledgeunlatched.org.

First published 2019
by Routledge
2 Park Square, Milton Park, Abingdon, Oxon OX14 4RN

and by Routledge
52 Vanderbilt Avenue, New York, NY 10017

Routledge is an imprint of the Taylor & Francis Group, an informa business

© 2019 Kim Barker and Olga Jurasz

The right of Kim Barker and Olga Jurasz to be identified as authors of this work has been asserted by them in accordance with sections 77 and 78 of the Copyright, Designs and Patents Act 1988.

The Open Access version of this book, available at www.taylorfrancis.com, has been made available under a Creative Commons Attribution-Non Commercial-No Derivatives 4.0 license.

Trademark notice: Product or corporate names may be trademarks or registered trademarks, and are used only for identification and explanation without intent to infringe.

British Library Cataloguing-in-Publication Data
A catalogue record for this book is available from the British Library

Library of Congress Cataloging-in-Publication Data
Names: Barker, Kim (Law teacher), author. |
Jurasz, Olga, author.
Title: Online misogyny as a hate crime: a challenge for legal regulation? / Kim Barker and Olga Jurasz.
Description: New York, NY: Routledge, 2018. | Includes index.
Identifiers: LCCN 2018044585 | ISBN 9781138590373 (hbk)
Subjects: LCSH: Libel and slander—Great Britain. | Hate crimes—Great Britain. | Misogyny—Great Britain. |
Internet—Law and legislation—Great Britain.
Classification: LCC KD7980 .B37 2018 |
DDC 345.41/0256—dc23
LC record available at https://lccn.loc.gov/2018044585

ISBN: 978-1-138-59037-3 (hbk)
ISBN: 978-0-429-95680-5 (ebk)

DOI: 10.4324/9780429956805

Typeset in Times New Roman
by codeMantra

For all the #badfeminists out there, we're with you!

Contents

Acknowledgments

This book would not have been possible without support from the Open University Strategic Research Area for funding that enabled completion of the research underpinning this project.

Thanks must go to Professor James Chalmers and Nicola Monaghan for their encouragement and for their many detailed and helpful comments on earlier parts of this work. Similarly, to Professor Rosa Freedman for her time and constructive critique at the early stages – nice one matey! To the anonymous reviewers also, your comments were highly insightful and helpful in the preparation of this work. To all at Routledge, but especially Siobhán Poole, your encouragement and enthusiasm was boundless in inspiring completion of the book, thank you.

We have also benefitted greatly from sharing research with the Cyberlaw stream of the Society of Legal Scholars Annual Conference (Dublin, 2017) and the discussion fostered by Dr Paul Bernal. Further thanks also to numerous other colleagues who have influenced this volume at various times.

In preparing the manuscript, the keen eye of Kevin Judge is hugely appreciated, as are the efforts of Craig Dalziel. Without their assistance, this volume would have been prepared long after the teaching term starts!

Finally, for the long hours, the endless cups of tea, and late-night FaceTime, globe-trotting, and accrued train miles (including rail replacement services!) from one co-author to another, #gotthereintheend!

KB & OJ
September 2018

Terminology

In general, a number of terms have been used both in the academic literature, and in the public domain more broadly, to describe various aspects of online abusive behaviour, including but not limited to online misogyny. However, some terms tend to be used interchangeably and sometimes even incorrectly, particularly where legal aspects of this subject come into play. This results in the production of a confused (as well as confusing) picture of what online misogyny is, what it entails, and which parts of the existing law (if any) apply to it. An unintended consequence of this is a narrow categorisation of online misogyny (and online abusive behaviour more broadly), for instance viewing it only as a form of cyberbullying or harassment to the exclusion of other (legal) aspects as well as categories which equally characterise it.

Throughout this book, various terms associated with issues of law, violence, hate, and misogyny are used. In order to provide readers with clarity on how these terms are applied here, the key terms, as understood by the authors for the purposes of this book, are listed and defined below.

Cyberstalking: involves the use of technology, predominantly the Internet, to make someone else afraid for, or concerned about, their safety. Such conduct is threatening or otherwise fear-inducing.[1]

Online harassment: a series of communications or sustained course of conduct involving written, electronic communications containing threatening and/or disruptive and/or distressing content.

1 Sameer Hinduja, 'Cyberstalking' (*Cyberbullying Research Center*, 21 March 2018) <https://cyberbullying.org/cyberstalking> accessed 10 September 2018.

Gender: socially constructed roles, behaviours, activities and attributes that a given society considers appropriate for women and men.

Gender-based hate: Prejudice or bias that is directed against a woman because she is a woman or that affects women disproportionately.

Misogyny: the manifestation of hostility towards women because they are women. For online misogyny, the manifestation of hostility communicated through online platforms, particularly social media and other participatory environments.

Online violence against women (OVAW) takes various forms of abuse and includes, but is not limited to, online misogyny, text-based abuse (e.g. on social media platforms such as Twitter or Facebook), upskirting, image-based sexual abuse (also referred to as 'revenge pornography'), rape pornography, doxing, cyberstalking and cyber-harassment.[2]

Violence against women (VAW) is understood as a violation of human rights and a form of discrimination against women and shall mean all acts of gender-based violence that result in, or are likely to result in, physical, sexual, psychological or economic harm or suffering to women, including threats of such acts, coercion or arbitrary deprivation of liberty, whether occurring in public or in private life (Istanbul Convention definition, Article 3).[3]

Social media abuse (SMA): written, electronic communication(s) posted on social media which contain(s) threatening and/or disruptive and/or distressing content and which fall(s) short of the thresholds for online harassment and online misogyny.

Text-based abuse (TBA): written, electronic communication containing threatening and/or disruptive and/or distressing content, such as, e.g., textual threats to kill, rape, or otherwise inflict harm on the recipient of such messages.

2 Kim Barker and Olga Jurasz, 'Submission of Evidence on Online Violence Against Women to the UN Special Rapporteur on Violence Against Women, its Causes and Consequences, Dr Dubravka Šimonović' (*Open University*, November 2017) <http://oro.open.ac.uk/52611/> accessed 10 September 2018.

3 Council of Europe Convention on Preventing and Combating Violence against Women and Domestic Violence (opened for signature 11 May 2011, entered into force 1 August 2014) (2011) CETS 210 (Istanbul Convention).

1 Misogyny

Law & the online feminist

'Women everywhere have had enough. We've reached our tipping point and we're not afraid to say it. We're not afraid to be dismissed, or belittled, or left out any more, because there are too many of us. There's no silencing someone who has tens of thousands of others standing right behind them. We can't be silenced when we're all saying the same thing.

A storm is coming. It didn't start out as a full-blown hurricane. It started with almost imperceptible whispers of 'is it just me?' and 'hang on a minute...' and 'maybe I'm overreacting, but...'.'

Laura Bates, Everyday Sexism.[1]

1.1 Introduction – why this book and why now

In recent years,[2] online misogyny has gained much international media coverage and attracted calls for urgent responses – from society, law, politics, platform regulators, and social media platforms alike – yet, little has been done to trigger meaningful and lasting change. However, where legal responses are concerned, the progress in addressing online misogyny has been slow. It also sorely lacks a comprehensive approach underpinned by a gender-based understanding of this phenomenon and an appreciation for the multiplicity of factors, actors, and, conditionalities which ought to be given due

1 Laura Bates, *Everyday Sexism* (Simon & Schuster 2014) 362.

2 Most recently, the Justice Minister, Lucy Frazer, committed to yet another review of hate crime laws, including – as a political trade-off – consideration of how sex and gender characteristics should be considered by new or existing hate crime laws. Libby Brooks, 'Review Brings Misogyny as a Hate Crime a Step Closer' *The Guardian* (London, 6 September 2018) <www.theguardian.com/society/2018/sep/05/first-step-to-misogyny-becoming-a-hate-called-amazing-victory> accessed 10 September 2018.

DOI: 10.4324/9780429956805-1

consideration in tackling online misogyny. Instead, law reform focuses on selective issues in tackling gender-based abuse online, particularly addressing image-based sexual abuse.[3] In contrast, online misogyny, which is typically expressed through text-based abuse on social media (e.g. hateful tweets directed at women), has remained outside the scope of legal regulation to date. Although various existing legal provisions could theoretically be used to make perpetrators of such abuse liable for their acts, these laws are largely outdated and not fit for purpose.[4] This is due to the fact that they largely precede the rise of digital society and, subsequently, the pandemic of online abusive behaviours. Furthermore, the sheer volume of *potentially* applicable legal provisions, compounded by the multiplicity of distinct tests unique to specific offences, as well as variations in terminology used to describe behaviours constituting a form of (online) abuse, result in a busy, confusing, and frequently contradictive legal landscape – one which ultimately fails to address the phenomenon of online misogyny and provide avenues for redress to its victims.

At the same time, whilst law and policy changes aimed at combatting online misogyny have been slow, recent years have seen an increase in academic engagements with the topic of gendered social media abuse and online misogyny. Writing across various disciplines, scholars have analysed online misogyny from a number of disciplinary angles, highlighting multiple aspects and implications of this global phenomenon – from tracing its history,[5] feminist resistance to online hate,[6] the impact on women's visibility in digital public spaces,[7] the symbolic nature of such forms of violence,[8] to the analysis of virtual

3 Clare McGlynn and Erika Rackley, 'Image-Based Sexual Abuse' (2017) 37 OJLS 534. Image-based sexual abuse is now regulated by law in England & Wales, Scotland, and Northern Ireland: Criminal Justice and Courts Act 2015, s 33; Abusive Behaviour and Sexual Harm (Scotland) Act 2016 (asp 22) s 2; Justice Act (Northern Ireland) 2016, ss 51 – 53.

4 As is demonstrated in Chapter 3 of this book.

5 Emma A Jane, *Misogyny Online: A Short (and Brutish) History* (SAGE 2017).

6 Jenny Sundén and Susanna Paasonen, 'Shameless Hags and Tolerance Whores: Feminist Resistance to the Affective Circuits of Online Hate' (2018) 18 Feminist Media Studies 643.

7 Sarah Sobieraj, 'Bitch, Slut, Skank, Cunt: Patterned Resistance to Women's Visibility in Digital Publics' (2017) 21 Information, Communication & Society 1700.

8 Karen Lumsden and Heather M Morgan, 'Cyber-trolling as Symbolic Violence: Deconstructing Gendered Abuse Online' in Nancy Lombard (ed) *The Routledge Handbook of Gender and Violence* (Routledge 2018).

manhood and its relationship with online misogyny.[9] However, such literature originates mostly from media and communications studies, sociology and, to an extent, criminology, leaving the *legal* perspective on this subject largely unexplored.

In light of these manifest gaps in the current legislative landscape and in the academic literature, this book is about how the law in England & Wales can, and ought to, respond to the phenomenon of online misogyny. The perspective presented here focuses on the legal, domestic response to this pressing global problem. Due to the constraints of this book, the arguments advanced here focus specifically on the law of England & Wales and, within that, the scope of criminal law in addressing online misogyny as hate crime. This book comes off the back of several years of authors' research into gender, online social media abuse and online violence against women.[10] This book offers an exploration of online misogyny through this particular lens which has been additionally encouraged by the recent developments in England, and in Scotland[11] which have called for making (online) misogyny a hate crime.

1.2 What this book is (not) about

This book makes a substantive, significant, and leading contribution to the growing literature on online misogyny and, given the scarcity of legal literature on this topic, aims to provide a legal analysis of this

9 Mairead E Moloney and Tony P Love, 'Assessing Online Misogyny: Perspectives from Sociology and Feminist Media Studies' (2018) 12(5) Sociology Compass e12577 <https://doi.org/10.1111/soc4.12577> accessed 10 September 2018.

10 Kim Barker and Olga Jurasz, 'Gender, Human Rights and Cybercrime: Are Virtual Worlds Really That Different?' in Michael Asimow, Kathryn Brown and David Ray Papke (eds), *Law and Popular Culture: International Perspectives* (Cambridge Scholars Publishing 2014); Kim Barker and Olga Jurasz, 'Submission of Evidence on Online Violence Against Women to the UN Special Rapporteur on Violence Against Women, its Causes and Consequences, Dr Dubravka Šimonović' (*Open University*, November 2017) <http://oro.open.ac.uk/52611/> accessed 10 September 2018; Kim Barker and Olga Jurasz, 'Submission of Evidence to Scottish Government Independent Review of Hate Crime Legislation (Bracadale Review)' (*Open University*, December 2017) <http://oro.open.ac.uk/52612/> accessed 10 September 2018; Kim Barker and Olga Jurasz, 'Written Submission of Evidence to the Women and Equalities Committee Inquiry into Sexual Harassment of Women and Girls in Public Spaces' (*Open University*, March 2018) <http://oro.open.ac.uk/53804/> accessed 10 September 2018.

11 Despite the focus of this book resting on England & Wales, occasional references will be made to developments in Scotland. These are mentioned because of Scotland's progressive outlook and ongoing efforts towards reforming the hate crime framework and addressing misogyny. See also Chapter 4.

modern phenomenon. It also proposes avenues for adequate legal responses, particularly within the realm of criminal law (and hate crime specifically) in England & Wales. In doing so, the book focuses on online misogyny which is manifested through social media, most notably the micro-blogging platform Twitter, in the form of text-based abuse (e.g. misogynistic tweets). However, online misogyny as a form of social media abuse is connected to a number of various interrelated issues and forms of online abuse. It is also not unique to Twitter despite its prevalence there – as such, the majority of examples referred to in this volume derive from this micro-blogging site rather than social media generally.

Frequently, although mistakenly, online misogyny is wrongly categorised under related, though distinct forms of online abuse, including image-based sexual abuse and cyberbullying.[12] Whilst the interrelatedness of these issues is noted, the book does not consider them in greater detail. Furthermore, the topic of online misogyny raises broader questions which are equally relevant to any (abusive) activity taking place on social media – including the matters concerning free speech, responsibilities of platform providers, and Internet jurisdiction. These are highlighted at various points in this book albeit not directly discussed in detail here.[13]

Although the authors acknowledge that misandry[14] also occurs on the Internet, the substantive analysis of this issue falls outside the remit of this book. This book is about *women*, their experiences of participating online, and the ultimate gender-bias of the law reflected in the lack of the appropriate legal remedies for women abused online. It is also concerned with the exclusion of women from this regulatory realm. Finally, it is to these women – who have experienced online misogyny, have been fighting against it, have been silenced by it, and who have been failed by the inadequate response of the current legal system – that we dedicate this book.

12 Communications Select Committee, *Social Media and Criminal Offences* (HL 2014 – 15, 37).

13 See discussions in Chapters 3 and 4.

14 Paul Nathanson and Katherine K Young, *Spreading Misandry: The Teaching of Contempt for Men in Popular Culture* (McGill-Queen's University Press 2001). For a contrasting view and a critical discussion on how the term misandry, used by the online manosphere, reinforces a misogynistic ontology which paints feminism as a man-hating movement, see Alice E Marwick and Robyn Caplan, 'Drinking Male Tears: Language, the Manosphere, and Networked Harassment' (2018) 18 Feminist Media Studies 543.

1.3 Addressing online misogyny through law: the limitations

> 'Well, it may be true that morality cannot be legislated but behaviour can be regulated. It may be true that the law cannot change the heart but it can restrain the heartless. It may be true that the law cannot make a man love me but it can restrain him from lynching me; and I think that is pretty important also. And so, while the law may not change the hearts of men, it does change the habits of men if it is vigorously enforced, and through changes in habits, pretty soon attitudinal changes will take place and even the heart may be changed in the process.'
>
> Martin Luther King Jr[15]

Online misogyny is a socio-cultural phenomenon and, as such, requires multidisciplinary input in order to accurately examine, understand, and tackle this problem. It is undisputable that the change in law alone is not sufficient to result in a meaningful change of social attitudes which, in cases of misogyny, have been shaped and maintained for centuries.[16] However, as it is argued in this book, the law has a significant role to play when it comes to influencing change in such behaviours online as well as providing meaningful avenues of redress for women who have been subjected to online misogyny, gender-based hate, and other forms of online abuse. Although legislation cannot change attitudes, it can increase awareness and give victims more confidence and, combined with other measures outside of the law, can contribute to a gradual, attitudinal change.

This book critically analyses the deficiencies in the current legal provisions on hate crime, advocating for a greater level of consistency across all sectors, but in particular the justice system. However, within the law itself, there are a number of issues which influence the way in

15 Martin Luther King Jr, 'Speech on Receipt of Honorary Doctorate in Civil Law' (*University of Newcastle upon Tyne*, 13 November 1967) <www.ncl.ac.uk/media/wwwnclacuk/congregations/files/Transcript%20of%20Dr%20Martin%20Luther%20King%20Jr%20speech%2013th%20November%201967.pdf> accessed 10 September 2018.

16 Andrea Nye, 'The Virtues of Misogyny' in Andrea Nye, *Feminism and Modern Philosophy: An Introduction* (Taylor & Francis Group, Routledge 2004) 12 – 33. See also Diana Coole, *Women in Political Theory: From Ancient Misogyny to Contemporary Feminism* (2nd rev edn, Prentice-Hall 1993).

which another area of the law (or a specific jurisdiction) can respond.[17] When it comes to online misogyny (or indeed any other form of online abuse), an additional two key factors arise: first, the issue of jurisdiction and the Internet and, second, the responsibility of platform providers for regulating and curtailing abusive behaviour occurring on their platforms, including online hate. Although this book does not examine these issues in depth, their relevance and the bearing they have on the ability of the law to meaningfully respond to online abuse and online hate are briefly explored below.[18]

1.3.1 Jurisdiction

The issue of jurisdiction in terms of the Internet represents a complicating factor when approaching the problem of hate online. In tackling any aspect of online hate, identifying the location of the 'harm' suffered, and the location of the perpetrator of that harm does not necessarily correlate to the same legal jurisdiction for mechanisms of redress. This problem is further compounded when suggestions of platform responsibility arise – notably for the 'Internet Giants,'[19] which operate across physical borders and across multiple legal juris-

17 Discussions in Chapter 3, 3.2. The limitation paradox explore such limitations, including those posed by Devolution and European Union law respectively.

18 Detailed discussions of this issue undoubtedly have a place but are outside the remit of this volume. But see, for example: David R Johnson and David G Post, 'Law and Borders – The Rise of Law in Cyberspace' (1996) 48 Stan L Rev 1367; Jack Goldsmith, 'Against Cyberanarchy' (1998) 65 U Chi L Rev 119; Joel R Reidenberg, 'Technology and Internet Jurisdiction' (2005) 153 U Pa L Rev 1951; Yee Fen Lim, *Cyberspace Law: Commentaries and Materials* (2nd edn, OUP 2007); Jack Goldsmith and Tim Wu, *Who Controls the Internet?: Illusions of a Borderless World* (OUP 2008); Jason T Kunze, 'Regulating Virtual Realms Optimally: The Model End User License Agreement' (2008) 7 Nw J Tech & Intell Prop 102; Thomas Schulz, 'Carving up the Internet: Legal Orders, and the Private/Public International Law Interface' (2008) 19 EJIL 799; Brendan J Gilbert, 'Getting to Conscionable: Negotiating Virtual Worlds' End User License Agreements without Getting Externally Regulated' (2009) 4 J Int'l Com L & Tech 238; Christopher T Marsden, *Net Neutrality: Towards a Co-Regulatory Solution* (Bloomsbury Academic 2010); Andrew Cabasso, 'Piercing Pennoyer with the Sword of a Thousand Truths: Jurisdictional Issues in the Virtual World' (2012) 22 Fordham Intell Prop Media & Ent LJ 383; Christopher GJ Morse, David McClean and Lawrence Collins, *Dicey, Morris & Collins on the Conflict of Laws* (15th edn, Sweet & Maxwell 2012); Chris Reed, *Making Laws for Cyberspace* (OUP 2012).

19 Notably Facebook, YouTube, Twitter and Microsoft. Arguably Google should be categorised here too but instances of online misogynistic abuse are less prevalent on search engines than on social media platforms.

dictions. A growing body of decisions relating to the potential liabilities and responsibilities of Internet service providers have been made by senior courts within England & Wales[20] and at a European level, which indicate – albeit controversially – the existence of a liability shield for providers at present.[21] Such shields operate as routes of obfuscation when it comes to accountability – if platform providers are not liable due to legal shields, then the only realistic route of redress falls back to acting against individuals – and this is a problem which has been encountered unsuccessfully in the context of file-sharing and copyright infringement.[22]

1.3.2 Platform regulation

Platform providers have a responsibility to ensure that their users are in compliance with their own codes of conduct. Beyond this, platform providers – including the so-called 'Internet Giants' – are not above the law, despite claims that cyberspace does not recognise attempts to control it.[23] Internet service providers – including platform providers – must therefore act in compliance with the law and act within it. The difficulty which often arises here is that the responsibilities often fall short of a legal obligation. Even where those responsibilities equate to a legal obligation, reporting and evidence gathering is extremely challenging, more so where the seizing of evidence has traditionally focussed on physical elements.[24] Therefore, many instances of online abuse perpetrated through social media platforms tend to fall short of the scope of the current legal provisions dealing with hate crime and abusive communications[25] – this is also notable in the lack of prosecutions and in the lack of statistical reporting in this area of crime. The occurrence of criminal liability for online abuse may provide an opportunity for greater success but will face some similar challenges to those encountered when attempting to deal with online file-sharing – notably in the identification of those users engaging in abusive

20 *R v Sheppard* [2010] EWCA Crim 65, [2010] 1 WLR 2779.

21 *Delfi AS v Estonia* App no 64569/09 (ECtHR, 16 June 2015).

22 Krzysztof Garstka, 'The Amended Digital Economy Act 2010 as an Unsuccessful Attempt to Solve the Stand-Alone Complex of Online Piracy' (2012) 43 IIC 158, 166.

23 John Perry Barlow, 'A Declaration of the Independence of Cyberspace' (*Electronic Frontier Foundation*, 8 February 1996) <https://www.eff.org/cyberspace-independence> accessed 10 September 2018.

24 Esther George and Stephen Mason, 'Obtaining Evidence from Mobile Devices and the Cloud' (2015) 21 CTLR 245.

25 See also Chapter 3.

behaviour if they are using anonymised social media accounts. This is a particularly important point because the anonymous nature of the online abuse and threats adds to the impact on those targeted.[26]

1.4 Feminism, law, and the fight against (online) misogyny

Feminist legal scholars have long demonstrated the gender-bias of the law and critiqued its neutrality and objectivity. Feminist critiques of the law that have developed from a variety of perspectives and representing various theoretical angles – from liberal to radical and post-modern feminists – subverted the perception of the alleged gender neutrality of the law. In particular, feminist legal scholars have questioned its gendered assumptions and challenged the role of the law and the (male) norms reflected in a way in which legal personality is characterised with the legal system.[27] For instance, a feminist critique of law unveiled and challenged the double standards that have long operated in the courtroom in that women's actions were measured by strikingly different criteria from those used to assess male conduct, especially, although not exclusively, in cases involving rape and sexual violence. As noted by Helena Kennedy, "rape cases became the central battleground"[28] in the feminist quest for the equal treatment of women within the law and by the law. The different treatment of women by, and in, the criminal justice system was also made strikingly visible in *R v Ahluwalia*[29] – a case demonstrating how the laws of self-defence and provocation in relation to murder were inherently biased against women and, ultimately, how the alleged 'gender blindness' of the law reinforced these inequalities on both substantive and procedural levels. Feminist (legal) writing and activism (e.g. the relentless campaigning efforts of Southall Black Sisters in Kiranjit Ahluwalia's case) also resulted in long overdue but substantive changes in the law – e.g. the House of Lords overturning the marital rape exemption

26 See also Chapter 3.

27 See generally: Carol Smart, *Feminism and the Power of Law* (Routledge 1989); Ngaire Naffine, 'Who are Law's Persons? From Cheshire Cats to Responsible Subjects' (2003) 66 MLR 346; Rosemary Hunter, 'Contesting the Dominant Paradigm: Feminist Critiques of Liberal Legalism' in Margaret Davies and Vanessa E Munro (eds), *The Ashgate Companion to Feminist Legal Theory* (Ashgate Publishing 2013).

28 Helena Kennedy, *Just Law: The Changing Face of Justice – and Why it Matters to Us All* (Chatto & Windus 2004) 171.

29 [1992] EWCA Crim 1.

under the English Law (*R v R* [1992]).[30] Furthermore, feminist legal scholars challenged the public-private divide in law and public policy, as demonstrated by the long-standing reluctance of the law to regulate the private sphere.[31] In highlighting the negative implications of such a dichotomy for women – particularly where domestic violence is involved – this has led to changes in the law, at both domestic and international levels, especially in the context of addressing violence against women as a human rights violation.[32] Importantly however, such a critique brought to light how such distinctions sustain the inequality and exploit the precarity of circumstances in which many women find themselves, as well as how the law reinforces such inequalities.

Despite many significant advances in overcoming various forms of inequality, both in private and public spheres, formal legal equality (e.g. in the form of the Equality Act 2010) has not translated into a long-term change of social attitudes towards women. Many battles fought by feminists in the late 1980s and 1990s, such as in relation to sexual harassment[33] and pornography, are still resonating in today's (digital) world. What has changed is the environment in which sexism and misogyny are expressed as well as forms in which they are directed against women.

Some forms of explicit discrimination, such as the exclusion of women from political suffrage, or from working in the legal profession, or from the receipt of unequal pay for equal work have been challenged and resulted in legal reform (and *de jure*, albeit not necessarily *de facto* equality). Despite this, gender inequality and misogyny continue to thrive – both within the law and in social attitudes. In the legal context, such manifestations can occur explicitly, for instance in the form of discriminatory laws or gender-biased applications of them. Moreover, it is frequently the silence of the law which points towards areas in which gender inequality is encouraged to flourish.[34]

However, the principles and efforts of the 'feminist legal project' are continually positioned against the forces of commonplace and

30 [1992] 1 AC 599.

31 Margaret Thornton, 'The Public/Private Dichotomy: Gendered and Discriminatory' (1991) 18 JLSoc'y 448; Susan B Boyd (ed) *Challenging the Public/Private Divide: Feminism, Law, and Public Policy* (University of Toronto Press 1997).

32 Alice Edwards, *Violence Against Women Under International Human Rights Law* (CUP 2011); Olga Jurasz, 'The Istanbul Convention: A New Chapter in Preventing and Combating Violence against Women' (2015) 89 ALJ 619.

33 See, for example: Catharine A MacKinnon, *Sexual Harassment of Working Women: A Case of Sex Discrimination* (Yale University Press 1976).

34 See also Chapter 2.

everyday misogyny, especially in the public sphere. Misogyny continues to thrive at the highest levels of political and public life and is expressed both online and offline. The notoriety of misogynistic tweets and comments expressed by the US President Donald Trump, misogynistic comments of the former MP Toby Young[35] and of the former Australian politician Tony Abbott (resulting in the PM, Julia Gillard, delivering a parliamentary speech on misogyny)[36] are just a few examples of behaviours which occur every day and are directed against women all over the world. However, whilst such expressions of misogyny attract some (short-lived) public critique – especially on social media – the lack of significant implications for those expressing such views contributes to the overall climate of legitimisation of misogynistic speech as well as a normalisation of such attitudes across the globe. The large scale, common, and public display of such behaviours are painful reminders that gender inequalities and misogyny not only continue to pervade social attitudes and the public sphere but are also frequently reinforced by law (and the legal system more broadly). This occurs despite equality and non-discrimination legislation being in existence. Irrespective of this, the law remains silent on the issue of misogyny, pushing it into the grey sphere of non-regulation. This in turn has implications for any efforts to combat online misogyny through the law. The persistent gendered assumptions about women participating online and the nature of misogynistic online abuse, as well as its impact, influence the manner in which the law is (not) responding to this pressing social issue. The following chapters of this book explore these conditionalities and demonstrate the shortcomings in the ways that the law in England & Wales has thus far failed to tackle gendered abuse online generally and online misogyny specifically.

1.5 The rise of the digital feminist

The emergence of the Internet and social media has had an immense impact on feminism and feminist activism. The Internet created an environment which, in principle, gave promise to the creation of a public

35 Kevin Rawlinson, 'Toby Young Faces Fresh Calls for his Sacking in Misogyny Row' *The Guardian* (London, 7 January 2018) <www.theguardian.com/media/2018/jan/07/toby-young-faces-fresh-calls-for-his-sacking-in-misogyny-row> accessed 10 September 2018.

36 Sydney Morning Herald, 'Transcript of Julia Gillard's Speech' *The Sydney Morning Herald* (Sydney, 10 October 2012) <www.smh.com.au/politics/federal/transcript-of-julia-gillards-speech-20121010-27c36.html> accessed 10 September 2018.

space – free, egalitarian, and open to all. Whilst the rise of online misogyny as well as other forms of social media abuse[37] has exposed and challenged the utopian ideal of this premise, online social media remain not only spaces of abuse, but also of resistance – particularly for feminists.

The rise of social media has opened up a space for feminists to organise, express solidarity, campaign and protest.[38] The online nature of such activities makes them public, open, and accessible beyond geographical borders. This has allowed for greater dissemination of feminist work, connecting feminists worldwide, culminating in the tentative emergence of the fourth wave of feminism[39] – a movement characterised by online activism. Noting the impact of the Internet on feminist activism over the past few decades, Jouët points towards some of the key characteristics of feminism online:

> Younger feminists are experts in using the technical and narrative frames of digital media and in developing innovative discourses. Furthermore, on the web, there is no limit for editorial content. The enormous number of feminist materials provided, daily and on an immediate and free access in the cyberspace, appears to be one of the major changes between activism in the seventies and in early 21st century.[40]

The use of social media for feminist campaigning and protest has also triggered a change in relation to the usual demographics of women engaged in feminist campaigning, including the increase in the use of Internet by girls who proclaim feminist viewpoints,[41] as well as the rise

37 Jesse Daniels, *Cyber Racism: White Supremacy Online and the New Attack on Civil Rights* (Rowman & Littlefield Publishers 2009); Imran Awan (ed), *Islamophobia in Cyberspace: Hate Crimes Go Viral* (Ashgate Publishing 2016); Moya Bailey and Trudy, 'On Misogynoir: Citation, Erasure, and Plagiarism' (2018) 18 Feminist Media Studies 762.

38 Kim Barker and Christina Baghdady, 'From Hybrid to Cybrid? The Formation and Regulation of Online 'Hybrid' Identities' in Nicolas Lemay-Hérbert and Rosa Freedman (eds), *Hybridity: Law, Culture and Development* (Routledge, 2017).

39 Ealasaid Munro, 'Feminism: A Fourth Wave?' (2013) 4 Political Insight 22. *The New York Times Magazine*

40 Josiane Jouët, *Digital Feminism: Questioning the Renewal of Activism* (Media@LSE Working Paper #48, Media@LSE 2017) <www.lse.ac.uk/media-and-communications/assets/documents/research/working-paper-series/WP48.pdf> accessed 10 September 2018, 8.

41 Sue Jackson, 'Young Feminists, Feminism and Digital Media' (2018) 28 Feminism & Psychology 32.

in participation by women who normally do not engage in political activism. Commenting on these unique shifts in the way in which feminist networks work, Baer observed that:

> (d)igital platforms offer great potential for broadly disseminating feminist ideas, shaping new modes of discourse about gender and sexism, connecting to different constituencies, and allowing creative modes of protest to emerge.[42]

Baer's observation rings particularly true in situations where feminist voices are suppressed in an 'offline'/local socio-cultural context or where more 'traditional/offline' means of campaigning and protest have been suppressed or proven less effective. This was particularly notable in the context of political events such as the Arab Spring, which witnessed women in Egypt, Tunisia, Libya, and Yemen taking to social media to campaign for political change.[43] As such, women have emerged as key social leaders of these revolutions – vigorously participating both online and offline – although their gains in terms of advancing gender equality and women's rights remain questionable.[44]

The Internet has also changed the ways in which feminists organise online using not only social media, but other online media and spaces too.[45] Using various # on Twitter, women created new spaces for feminist momentum and solidarity whilst transcending national borders. For instance, in 2014, an Iranian journalist, Masih Alinejad created an online social movement #MyStealthyFreedom. Using the Facebook website of the movement as well as Twitter, Iranian women share photos of themselves not wearing the hijab in a protest against the imposition of the hijab by the Iranian authorities since the Iranian

42 Hester Baer, 'Redoing Feminism: Digital Activism, Body Politics, and Neoliberalism' (2016) 16 Feminist Media Studies 17, 18.

43 See, for example: Victoria A Newsom and Lara Lengel, 'Arab Women, Social Media, and the Arab Spring: Applying the Framework of Digital Reflexivity to Analyze Gender and Online Activism' (2012) 13(5) Journal of International Women's Studies 31; Barker and Baghdady, 'From Hybrid to Cybrid?' (n 38).

44 Olga Jurasz, 'Women of the Revolution: The Future of Women's Rights in Post-Gaddafi Libya' in Carlo Panara and Gary Wilson (eds), *The Arab Spring: New Patterns for Democracy and International Law* (Martinus Nijhoff Publishers 2013).

45 Alma Hassoun, ''We Are Real': Saudi Feminists Launch Online Radio' (*BBC News*, 19 August 2018) <www.bbc.com/news/world-middle-east-45181505> accessed 10 September 2018.

Revolution of 1979.[46] In 2016, Saudi women launched an online campaign on Twitter to end the guardianship system in Saudi Arabia (#TogetherToEndMaleGuardianship, #IAmMyOwnGuardian) having earlier (2011) protested against the driving ban by posting videos on YouTube and on Twitter picturing themselves driving cars during the #women2drive campaign.[47]

Social media has also become a space for raising awareness about the scale and the everyday nature of women's experiences of sexism, (sexual) violence, and misogyny. Campaigns such as #metoo allowed women to share personal accounts and experiences of sexual harassment and sexual abuse. Similarly, the *Everyday Sexism* project,[48] started by Laura Bates, has been documenting an overwhelming number of examples of sexism experienced by women in their everyday lives, which serve as worrying reminders, as well as evidence of the normalisation of sexist and misogynistic behaviours. Such campaigns have been notable, not least for enabling public and mass speaking out against sexual abuse and sexism on an unprecedented scale. Significantly, they also helped to erode "the two biggest barriers to ending sexual harassment in law and in life: the disbelief and trivializing dehumanization of its victims"[49] – something that legal provisions alone have not been able to achieve and consistently fail to address.

However, there has been a considerable backlash to feminist participation and campaigning online with the common experience of gender issues being trolled, ridiculed or pathologised when they appear on social media.[50] Similarly, raising online misogyny as an issue has also become susceptible to violent, hateful, and discriminatory

46 Facebook: 'My Stealthy Freedom' <https://www.facebook.com/StealthyFreedom> accessed 10 September 2018; Twitter: @masipooyan; Website: My Stealthy Freedom <http://mystealthyfreedom.net/en/> accessed 10 September 2018.

47 Nora Doaiji, 'Saudi Women's Online Activism: One Year of the "I Am My Own Guardian" Campaign' (*The Arab Gulf States Institute in Washington*, 19 October 2017) <https://agsiw.org/saudi-womens-online-activism-one-year-guardian-campaign/> accessed 10 September 2018.

48 Everyday Sexism Project <https://everydaysexism.com> accessed 10 September 2018. See also Twitter: @EverydaySexism, #everydaysexism.

49 Catharine A MacKinnon, '#MeToo Has Done What the Law Could Not' *The New York Times* (New York, 4 February 2018) <www.nytimes.com/2018/02/04/opinion/metoo-law-legal-system.htmlaccessed> 10 September 2018.

50 Abigail Locke, Rebecca Lawthom, and Antonia Lyons, 'Social Media Platforms as Complex Spaces for Feminisms: Visibility, Opportunity, Power, Resistance and Activism' (2018) 28 Feminism & Psychology 3, 4.

responses, both offline and online. Similar reactions have been observed in relation to the dissemination of feminist research[51] as well as research on oppressed groups – most especially when it is shared on social media.[52] The increase in online violence against women and the trolling of women – as well as online misogyny – has led to the establishment of a number of (predominantly feminist) organisations and campaigns[53] calling for combatting OVAW and making the Internet free of (gendered) abuse.

Whilst the work of organisations such as Reclaim the Internet is crucial in campaigning for change and in raising awareness of various forms of OVAW, there has been very little substantive change – neither in law nor policy – aimed at addressing these issues. Furthermore, continued misogyny, as well as the targeting of women online is also demonstrative of how little has happened in terms of socio-cultural and attitudinal change, despite the work done by feminist groups and activists.

Some changes, e.g. in terms of advancing equality law, have taken place, yet the lasting attitudinal/cultural change has been slow, and victories, few and far between. As this book demonstrates, the law is in dire need of reform in order to respond to gender-based abuse online. Most desperately, it must start treating such abuse as an obstacle to the participation of women in public (online) spaces.

Bibliography

Table of cases

England & Wales
R v Ahluwalia [1992] EWCA Crim 1
R v R [1992] 1 AC 599
R v Sheppard [2010] EWCA Crim 65, [2010] 1 WLR 2779

51 Fiona Vera-Gray, ''Talk About a Cunt with Too Much Idle Time': Trolling Feminist Research' (2017) 115 Feminist Review 61.

52 Charlotte Barlow and Imran Awan, '"You Need to Be Sorted Out With a Knife": The Attempted Online Silencing of Women and People of Muslim Faith Within Academia' (2016) 2 Social Media + Society 1.

53 Examples include: Glitch!UK <https://seyiakiwowo.com/GlitchUK/> accessed 10 September 2018; Luchadoras <https://luchadoras.mx/category/internet-feminista/> accessed 10 September 2018; Reclaim the Internet <http://www.reclaimtheinternet.com> accessed 10 September 2018; Take Back the Tech <https://www.takebackthetech.net> accessed 10 September 2018; Women, Action, & the Media (WAM!) <http://womenactionmedia.org> accessed 10 September 2018.

European Court of Human Rights

Delfi AS v Estonia App no 64569/09 (ECtHR, 16 June 2015)

Table of legislation

UK Public General Acts

Criminal Justice and Courts Act 2015

Acts of the Scottish Parliament

Abusive Behaviour and Sexual Harm (Scotland) Act 2016 (asp 22)

Acts of the Northern Ireland Assembly

Justice Act (Northern Ireland) 2016

List of secondary sources

Books

Awan I (ed), *Islamophobia in Cyberspace: Hate Crimes Go Viral* (Ashgate Publishing 2016)

Bates L, *Everyday Sexism* (Simon & Schuster 2014)

Boyd SB (ed), *Challenging the Public/Private Divide: Feminism, Law, and Public Policy* (University of Toronto Press 1997)

Coole D, *Women in Political Theory: From Ancient Misogyny to Contemporary Feminism* (2nd rev edn, Prentice-Hall 1993)

Daniels J, *Cyber Racism: White Supremacy Online and the New Attack on Civil Rights* (Rowman & Littlefield Publishers 2009)

Edwards A, *Violence Against Women Under International Human Rights Law* (CUP 2011)

Goldsmith J and Wu T, *Who Controls the Internet?: Illusions of a Borderless World* (OUP 2008)

Jane EA, *Misogyny Online: A Short (and Brutish) History* (SAGE 2017)

Kennedy H, *Just Law: The Changing Face of Justice – and Why it Matters to Us All* (Chatto & Windus 2004)

Lim YF, *Cyberspace Law: Commentaries and Materials* (2nd edn, OUP 2007)

MacKinnon CA, *Sexual Harassment of Working Women: A Case of Sex Discrimination* (Yale University Press 1976)

Marsden CT, *Net Neutrality: Towards a Co-Regulatory Solution* (Bloomsbury Academic 2010)

Morse CGJ, McClean D and Collins L, *Dicey, Morris & Collins on the Conflict of Laws* (15th edn, Sweet & Maxwell 2012)

Nathanson P and Young KK, *Spreading Misandry: The Teaching of Contempt for Men in Popular Culture* (McGill-Queen's University Press 2001)

Nye A, *Feminism and Modern Philosophy: An Introduction* (Taylor & Francis Group, Routledge 2004)

Reed C, *Making Laws for Cyberspace* (OUP 2012)

Smart C, *Feminism and the Power of Law* (Routledge 1989)

Contributions to Edited Books

Barker K and Baghdady C, 'From Hybrid to Cybrid? The Formation and Regulation of Online 'Hybrid' Identities' in Lemay-Hérbert N and Freedman R (eds), *Hybridity: Law, Culture and Development* (Routledge, 2017)

Barker K and Jurasz O, 'Gender, Human Rights and Cybercrime: Are Virtual Worlds Really That Different?' in Asimow M, Brown K and Papke DR (eds), *Law and Popular Culture: International Perspectives* (Cambridge Scholars Publishing 2014)

Hunter R, 'Contesting the Dominant Paradigm: Feminist Critiques of Liberal Legalism' in Margaret Davies and Vanessa E Munro (eds), *The Ashgate Companion to Feminist Legal Theory* (Ashgate Publishing 2013)

Jurasz O, 'Women of the Revolution: The Future of Women's Rights in Post-Gaddafi Libya' in Carlo Panara and Gary Wilson (eds), *The Arab Spring: New Patterns for Democracy and International Law* (Martinus Nijhoff Publishers 2013)

Lumsden K and Morgan HM, 'Cyber-trolling as Symbolic Violence: Deconstructing Gendered Abuse Online' in Lombard N (ed) *The Routledge Handbook of Gender and Violence* (Routledge 2018)

Evidence Submissions

Barker K and Jurasz O, 'Submission of Evidence on Online Violence Against Women to the UN Special Rapporteur on Violence Against Women, its Causes and Consequences, Dr Dubravka Šimonović' (*Open University*, November 2017) <http://oro.open.ac.uk/52611/> accessed 10 September 2018

———, 'Submission of Evidence to Scottish Government Independent Review of Hate Crime Legislation (Bracadale Review)' (*Open University*, December 2017) <http://oro.open.ac.uk/52612/> accessed 10 September 2018

———, 'Written Submission of Evidence to the Women and Equalities Committee Inquiry into Sexual Harassment of Women and Girls in Public Spaces' (*Open University*, March 2018) <http://oro.open.ac.uk/53804/> accessed 10 September 2018

Journal Articles

Baer H, 'Redoing Feminism: Digital Activism, Body Politics, and Neoliberalism' (2016) 16 Feminist Media Studies 17

Bailey M and Trudy, 'On Misogynoir: Citation, Erasure, and Plagiarism' (2018) 18 Feminist Media Studies 762

Barlow C and Awan I, '"You Need to Be Sorted Out With a Knife": The Attempted Online Silencing of Women and People of Muslim Faith Within Academia' (2016) 2 Social Media + Society 1

Cabasso A, 'Piercing Pennoyer with the Sword of a Thousand Truths: Jurisdictional Issues in the Virtual World' (2012) 22 Fordham Intell Prop Media & Ent LJ 383

Garstka K, 'The Amended Digital Economy Act 2010 as an Unsuccessful Attempt to Solve the Stand-Alone Complex of Online Piracy' (2012) 43 IIC 158

George E and Mason S, 'Obtaining Evidence from Mobile Devices and the Cloud' (2015) 21 CTLR 245

Gilbert BJ, 'Getting to Conscionable: Negotiating Virtual Worlds' End User License Agreements without Getting Externally Regulated' (2009) 4 J Int'l Com L & Tech 238

Goldsmith J, 'Against Cyberanarchy' (1998) 65 U Chi L Rev 119

Jackson S, 'Young Feminists, Feminism and Digital Media' (2018) 28 Feminism & Psychology 32

Johnson DR and Post DG, 'Law and Borders – The Rise of Law in Cyberspace' (1996) 48 Stan L Rev 1367

Jurasz O, 'The Istanbul Convention: A New Chapter in Preventing and Combating Violence against Women' (2015) 89 ALJ 619

Kunze JT, 'Regulating Virtual Realms Optimally: The Model End User License Agreement' (2008) 7 Nw J Tech & Intell Prop 102

Locke A, Lawthom R and Lyons A, 'Social Media Platforms as Complex Spaces for Feminisms: Visibility, Opportunity, Power, Resistance and Activism' (2018) 28 Feminism & Psychology 3

Marwick AE and Caplan R, 'Drinking Male Tears: Language, the Manosphere, and Networked Harassment' (2018) 18 Feminist Media Studies 543

McGlynn C and Rackley E, 'Image-Based Sexual Abuse' (2017) 37 OJLS 534

Moloney ME and Love TP, 'Assessing Online Misogyny: Perspectives from Sociology and Feminist Media Studies' (2018) 12(5) Sociology Compass e12577 <https://doi.org/10.1111/soc4.12577> accessed 10 September 2018

Munro E, 'Feminism: A Fourth Wave?' (2013) 4 Political Insight 22

Naffine N, 'Who are Law's Persons? From Cheshire Cats to Responsible Subjects' (2003) 66 MLR 346

Newsom VA and Lengel L, 'Arab Women, Social Media, and the Arab Spring: Applying the Framework of Digital Reflexivity to Analyze Gender and Online Activism' (2012) 13(5) Journal of International Women's Studies 31

Reidenberg JR, 'Technology and Internet Jurisdiction' (2005) 153 U Pa L Rev 1951

Schulz T, 'Carving up the Internet: Legal Orders, and the Private/Public International Law Interface' (2008) 19 EJIL 799

Sobieraj S, 'Bitch, Slut, Skank, Cunt: Patterned Resistance to Women's Visibility in Digital Publics' (2017) 21 Information, Communication & Society 1700

Sundén J and Paasonen S, 'Shameless Hags and Tolerance Whores: Feminist Resistance to the Affective Circuits of Online Hate' (2018) 18 Feminist Media Studies 643

Thornton M, 'The Public/Private Dichotomy: Gendered and Discriminatory' (1991) 18 JLSoc'y 448

Vera-Gray F, "Talk About a Cunt with Too Much Idle Time': Trolling Feminist Research' (2017) 115 Feminist Review 61

Newspaper Articles

Brooks L, 'Review Brings Misogyny as a Hate Crime a Step Closer' *The Guardian* (London, 6 September 2018) <www.theguardian.com/society/2018/sep/05/first-step-to-misogyny-becoming-a-hate-called-amazing-victory> accessed 10 September 2018

MacKinnon CA, '#MeToo Has Done What the Law Could Not' *The New York Times* (New York, 4 February 2018) <www.nytimes.com/2018/02/04/opinion/metoo-law-legal-system.htmlaccessed> 10 September 2018

Rawlinson K, 'Toby Young Faces Fresh Calls for his Sacking in Misogyny Row' *The Guardian* (London, 7 January 2018) <www.theguardian.com/media/2018/jan/07/toby-young-faces-fresh-calls-for-his-sacking-in-misogyny-row> accessed 10 September 2018

Solomon D, 'Fourth-Wave Feminism' *The New York Times Magazine* (New York, 13 November 2009) <www.nytimes.com/2009/11/15/magazine/15fob-q4-t.html> accessed 10 September 2018

Sydney Morning Herald, 'Transcript of Julia Gillard's Speech' *The Sydney Morning Herald* (Sydney, 10 October 2012) <www.smh.com.au/politics/federal/transcript-of-julia-gillards-speech-20121010-27c36.html> accessed 10 September 2018

Parliamentary Reports

Communications Select Committee, *Social Media and Criminal Offences* (HL 2014 – 15, 37)

Social Media Platforms

Facebook

'My Stealthy Freedom' <https://www.facebook.com/StealthyFreedom> accessed 10 September 2018

Twitter

@EverydaySexism

#everydaysexism

@masipooyan

Websites

Barlow JP, 'A Declaration of the Independence of Cyberspace' (*Electronic Frontier Foundation*, 8 February 1996) <https://www.eff.org/cyberspace-independence> accessed 10 September 2018

Doaiji N, 'Saudi Women's Online Activism: One Year of the "I Am My Own Guardian" Campaign' (*The Arab Gulf States Institute in Washington*, 19 October 2017) <https://agsiw.org/saudi-womens-online-activism-one-year-guardian-campaign/> accessed 10 September 2018

Everyday Sexism Project <https://everydaysexism.com> accessed 10 September 2018

Glitch!UK <https://seyiakiwowo.com/GlitchUK/> accessed 10 September 2018

Hassoun A, "We Are Real': Saudi Feminists Launch Online Radio' (*BBC News*, 19 August 2018) <www.bbc.com/news/world-middle-east-45181505> accessed 10 September 2018

King Jr ML, 'Speech on Receipt of Honorary Doctorate in Civil Law' (*University of Newcastle upon Tyne*, 13 November 1967) <www.ncl.ac.uk/media/wwwnclacuk/congregations/files/Transcript%20of%20Dr%20Martin%20Luther%20King%20Jr%20speech%2013th%20November%201967.pdf> accessed 10 September 2018

Luchadoras <https://luchadoras.mx/category/internet-feminista/> accessed 10 September 2018

My Stealthy Freedom <http://mystealthyfreedom.net/en/> accessed 10 September 2018

Reclaim the Internet <http://www.reclaimtheinternet.com> accessed 10 September 2018

Take Back the Tech <https://www.takebackthetech.net> accessed 10 September 2018

Women, Action, & the Media (WAM!) <http://womenactionmedia.org> accessed 10 September 2018

Working Papers

Jouët J, *Digital Feminism: Questioning the Renewal of Activism* (Media@LSE Working Paper #48, Media@LSE 2017) <www.lse.ac.uk/media-and-communications/assets/documents/research/working-paper-series/WP48.pdf> accessed 10 September 2018

2 Online misogyny

Old problems, new media?

> The longer the content stays available, the more damage it can inflict on the victims and empower the perpetrators. If you remove the content at an early stage you can limit the exposure. This is just like cleaning litter, it doesn't stop people from littering but if you do not take care of the problem it just piles up and further exacerbates.
>
> Andre Oboler, CEO of the Online Hate Prevention Institute.[1]

2.1 Introduction – an open, participatory ideal?

The ideal of an open, all-inclusive, and participatory Internet has been undermined by the rise of misogynistic abuse on social media platforms. Despite the plethora of evidence illustrating how widespread this now is, responses have been rather stagnant. In England, the tackling of underlying causes of online abuse has been overlooked, predominantly because the criminal justice system is designed to react to social phenomena, and this has inevitably meant that the emphasis falls on changing perceptions before changing the law. Furthermore, online abuse has a significant impact on its victims that is underestimated by policymakers and subject to misperceptions that the online is not 'real'. As such, legal efforts to tackle online misogyny have to date been largely ineffective, ignored, and even where alluded to, not successful.

There is a pressing need for greater recognition of online harms within the legal system, but also socially. Specifically, in the most-high profile of cases concerning online misogyny and social media

1 Iginio Gagliardone and others, *Countering Online Hate Speech* (UNESCO 2015) <http://unesdoc.unesco.org/images/0023/002332/233231e.pdf> accessed 10 September 2018, 13.

DOI: 10.4324/9780429956805-2

abuse, the lower courts have shown themselves to be willing to give judicial recognition to non-traditional harms – typically in unreported cases such as *R v Nimmo and Sorley* (2014)[2] and *R v Viscount St Davids* (2017).[3] These non-traditional harms – including economic harm, residential harm, social harm, and psychological harm – stand in stark contrast with traditionally recognised criminal harms which appear in established legal authorities from senior courts, including *DPP v Collins* [2006],[4] and, more recently, *Chambers v DPP* [2012].[5] Despite these minor shifts, there has been very little recognition given to non-traditional harms – and their impact – by the judicial system; by the prosecution service;[6] and by the legislative organs. This chapter will demonstrate why this approach remains flawed.[7]

This chapter will outline the rise in social media use and abuse, commenting on the continuation of misogyny, albeit in a new context, as it is perpetrated through a new medium. In discussing this social phenomenon, this chapter will rely upon illustrations from recent examples to demonstrate the shift from offline misogyny to online misogyny. The discussion here will demonstrate that the perceptions surrounding misogyny are misplaced and will highlight the cumulative effects of online misogyny, offering a compelling portrayal of the impact such abuse can have, before leading to discussions outlining the legislative gaps which compound failings in this area. Essentially, the combined failures and cumulative impacts upon victims of online social media abuse provide a compelling basis from which to advocate for systemic change.

2.2 Social media abuse as a modern phenomenon

The changes in use of the Internet, and the increased number of engaged participants has led to a huge expansion in the last decade. The Internet at its origin was not designed to be dominated by participatory 'social' platforms – despite its communicatory beginnings[8] – that

2 *R v Nimmo and Sorley* (Westminster Magistrates' Court, 24 January 2014).
3 *R v Viscount St Davids* (Westminster Magistrates' Court, 11 July 2017).
4 *DPP v Collins* [2006] UKHL 40.
5 *Chambers v DPP* [2012] EWHC 2157 (Admin). For further discussion, see Chapter 3 – 3.4. Threats and Threats to Kill.
6 BBC News, 'Stalking reports treble as prosecution rates fall' (*BBC News*, 20 July 2018) <www.bbc.co.uk/news/uk-england-44887574> accessed 10 September 2018.
7 See discussions of legislative provisions in Chapter 3.
8 Paul Baran, 'On a Distributed Command and Control System Configuration' (RAND, 31 December 1960) <www.rand.org/content/dam/rand/pubs/research_memoranda/

encourage engagement to the point of addiction.[9] Digital detoxing, for example, is growing in importance – especially with the increase in the numbers of millennials having concerns about the amount of time they spend on social media[10] – and has become the subject of public health initiatives.[11] However, given the developments of the Internet to a position where the online and offline are increasingly blurred, the notion continues to exist that there are few repercussions for online actions. It is now more apparent than ever that there are consequences for particular behaviour online – in both online and offline forms. This is notable from jurisprudence dealing with image-based sexual abuse,[12] online defamation,[13] and terrorism.[14] What is less apparent however, is a recognition of the consequences that will follow from online misogynistic behaviours. To date, there have been only a few high-profile instances where significant attention has been given to the causes. This not only belittles the impact of social media abuse but is insulting to the numerous victims whose cases are not acted upon, or do not make the news headlines. Yet, the consequences and impact for these victims is as serious as for those victims who are 'high-profile'.

Online platforms – particularly social media platforms – are the digital equivalents of offline public places. As such, the same laws apply across both. The misperception that there will be immunity for online actions needs challenging generally – but especially here in the context of misogynistic abuse. There is a complete lack of recognition of the problem, but also of the harm that it can cause – a point summarised by the House of Lords in 2015, which compounded the

2009/RM2632.pdf> accessed 10 September 2018; Johnny Ryan, *A History of the Internet and the Digital Future (*Reaktion Books 2010) 15.

9 Rebecca Flood, 'Users Fear Social Media is Making Them Ill, but They Still Can't Stop' *The Independent* (London, 26 February 2017) <www.independent.co.uk/news/world/americas/smartphone-social-media-apps-mental-health-negative-check-plugged-in-communication-technology-a7600686.html> accessed 10 September 2018.

10 APA, 'Stress in America: Coping with Change' (10th edn, American Psychological Association 2017) <www.apa.org/news/press/releases/stress/2016/coping-with-change.PDF> accessed 10 September 2018.

11 RSPH, 'RSPH Announces 'Scroll Free September' Campaign to Improve Mental Health and Wellbeing' (*Royal Society for Public Health*, 27 July 2018) <www.rsph.org.uk/about-us/news/rsph-announces-scroll-free-september-campaign-to-improve-mental-health-and-wellbeing.html> accessed 10 September 2018.

12 Criminal Justice and Courts Act 2015, ss 32–35.

13 *McAlpine v Bercow* [2013] EWHC 1342 (QB).

14 *Chambers* (n 5).

recognition problem.[15] This misperception is difficult to understand because there are other areas of daily life which are highly regulated online – including banking,[16] online shopping,[17] and online security.[18] For all of these areas – and more – there are detailed legal provisions in place regulating every aspect. Yet, when it comes to instances of online misogyny and online text-based abuses, the regulatory system is less forthcoming. Such behaviour – unacceptable behaviour – is not just an online problem, it is very much a social problem.[19] In part this means that misogyny is deeply rooted in society – particularly offline society. That said, it is also deeply embedded in online society too – and it is difficult to challenge in a piecemeal manner the laissez-faire attitude to this cultural acceptance of a problem that is encroaching on everyday life. When children are exposed to sexism in school classrooms,[20] and political appointees to high-level posts have histories of such behaviours and continue to display such behaviours on a shockingly frequent basis,[21] it suggests that such attitudes are endemic. That does not mean however that such behaviour and attitudes ought to remain social norms and continue to be accepted. In terms of dealing with this, and other problems, social media platforms have shown themselves to be unwilling, or unable, to act. This has led to situations where legislators are suggesting punitive measures to attempt to engage the social media

15 Communications Select Committee, *Social Media and Criminal Offences* (HL 2014–15, 37).

16 See, for example, Banking Act 2009; Commission, 'Proposal for a Directive of the European Parliament and of the Council on Combating Fraud and Counterfeiting of Non-Cash Means of Payment and Replacing Council Framework Decision 2001/413/JHA' COM (2017) 489 final.

17 Consumer Rights Act 2015.

18 Regulation (EU) 2016/679 of the European Parliament and of the Council of 27 April 2016 on the protection of natural persons with regard to the processing of personal data and on the free movement of such data, and repealing Directive 95/46/EC (General Data Protection Regulation) (GDPR).

19 Amanda Hess, 'Why Women Aren't Welcome on the Internet' (*Pacific Standard*, 6 January 2014) <https://psmag.com/social-justice/women-arent-welcome-internet-72170> accessed 10 September 2018.

20 Laura Bates, 'Sexism in Schools is Real – How Can the Department for Education Deny It?' *The Guardian* (London, 31 March 2016) <https://www.theguardian.com/commentisfree/2016/mar/31/sexism-schools-department-of-education-deny-sexist-bullying> accessed 10 September 2018.

21 Kevin Rawlinson, 'Toby Young Faces Fresh Calls for his Sacking in Misogyny Row' *The Guardian* (London, 7 January 2018) <www.theguardian.com/media/2018/jan/07/toby-young-faces-fresh-calls-for-his-sacking-in-misogyny-row> accessed 10 September 2018.

platforms in addressing their responsibilities.[22] Similarly, the endemic, embedded nature of misogyny in public life means that it is very difficult for any strategies designed to combat misogyny to be truly effective. This situation is damaging to all women, but most especially to those who have been victimised by the perpetrators of misogyny. More so when the divide between the online and offline is crossed, and online misogynistic abuse takes on a physical form. There are serious consequences here. Worryingly, these consequences can materialise from the digital realm into the physical world because online platforms are no different to offline public spaces. Cooper summarises this adequately, stating that: "[w]e have responsibilities as online citizens to make sure the internet is a safe space."[23] The implications of misogynistic abuse being tolerated, accepted or even encouraged online are severe, going beyond name calling, cyberbullying, and e-Bile – leading to harassment, stalking, death and rape threats, and even murder.[24] As online citizens, we are failing double-fold. First, we are failing to ensure that the Internet is a safe space and, despite the evident fallibility of the online sphere, we are, second, failing to challenge, and be critical of, established, embedded norms. Consequently, women everywhere continue to live with the implications of this legacy.

2.3 From offline to online: the digital misogyny 'switch'

Misogyny as a phenomenon is not new – it has a persistent presence and takes a number of different forms, irrespective of medium. Traditionally, misogyny has been present in offline, personal, and physical interactions. However, in recent years, with the spread of technology and mobile Internet, the online realm, too, is providing a home for online misogynistic behaviours. Whilst these may have traditionally been found within male-dominated gaming environments,[25] the Internet is now much more

22 Home Affairs Committee, *Hate Crime: Abuse, Hate and Extremism Online* (HC 2016–17, 609); Owen Bowcott, 'Social Media Firms Must Face Heavy Fines over Extremist Content – MPs' *The Guardian* (London, 1 May 2017) <www.theguardian.com/media/2017/may/01/social-media-firms-should-be-fined-for-extremist-content-say-mps-google-youtube-facebook> accessed 10 September 2018.

23 Hardeep Matharu, 'Reclaim the Internet Campaign to Tackle 'Colossal' Scale of Online Misogyny' *The Independent* (London, 26 May 2016) <www.independent.co.uk/news/uk/home-news/research-reveals-colossal-scale-of-online-misogyny-a7049396.html> accessed 10 September 2018.

24 This discussion is continued below at 2.3.1. The normalisation of online abuse.

25 Dan Golding and Leena van Deventer, *Game Changers: From Minecraft to Misogyny, the Fight for the Future of Videogames* (Affirm Press 2016). See also, Jatinder

developed and open, and so too is misogyny. It is also much more prevalent. Online misogyny is a modern trend which overwhelmingly characterises women's experiences of participating online. Put simply, online misogyny is a form of gender-based cyberhate, directed against women because they are women. This 'new form of old misogyny'[26] affects women of all backgrounds who participate actively online – typically, although not exclusively, in situations where they express their views online and commonly where these opinions represent a feminist or otherwise not mainstream viewpoint. A study from 2016 indicates – alarmingly – that in a three-week period, 6500 social media users were targeted by 10 000 aggressive, explicit, and misogynistic tweets.[27] On a similar scale, at an international level, this is the equivalent of 80 000 users receiving 200 000 tweets which were similarly aggressive, hostile, and misogynistic.[28]

This is one dimension of the growing – pernicious and damaging – misogyny phenomenon. The other element to it, is not just the backlash that is directed against women online, but the torrent of abuse that is unleashed when women express opinions online. Although there are no worldwide studies on online misogyny, research from the UK and Europe indicates a large – and increasingly widening – scale of online violence against women (including online misogyny). It also highlights the effects of such acts on the victims. These findings are not isolated, with both national and international reports revealing similar conclusions. For instance, a 2017 report by Amnesty International exposed a concerning scale of online abuse and harassment of women and the alarming impact of such acts. A poll which looked at the experiences of women between the ages of 18 and 55 in Denmark, Italy, New Zealand, Poland, Spain, Sweden, the UK and USA demonstrated that nearly a quarter (23%) of surveyed women had experienced online abuse or harassment at least once.[29] Similarly, the UK 2016 Girlguiding Girls Attitude Survey indicated that 49% of girls, aged between 11 and 16,

Singh Nandra, 'The Dark Side of Gaming: "I've Been Called a Curry Muncher…"' (*BBC Three*, 7 March 2018) <https://www.bbc.co.uk/bbcthree/article/9fe76f89-2d48-4393-bbdd-d6b15b0b0503> accessed 10 September 2018.

26 Emma A Jane, *Misogyny Online: A Short (and Brutish) History* (SAGE 2017) 4.

27 Demos, 'The Use of Misogynistic Terms on Twitter' (*Demos*, 2016) <www.demos.co.uk/wp-content/uploads/2016/05/Misogyny-online.pdf> accessed 10 September 2018.

28 ibid.

29 Amnesty International, 'Amnesty Reveals Alarming Impact of Online Abuse against Women' (*Amnesty International*, 20 November 2017) <www.amnesty.org/en/latest/news/2017/11/amnesty-reveals-alarming-impact-of-online-abuse-against-women/> accessed 10 September 2018.

who were surveyed felt unable to express their views in an online environment.[30] This drops slightly – to 44% of those surveyed – in the 17–21 age category. Beyond that – and the truly damning statistic here – half of all women aged between 11 and 21 think sexism is worse online than it is offline. Whilst these studies are relatively small scale, this is a stark indicator of the damage being done to young women who seek equal participation in an online environment. This is particularly important in an increasingly digital and connected society, especially one where there has been a 51% rise in smartphone ownership over the last decade. In 2008, only 17% of adults in the UK owned a smartphone – that figure is now 78%[31] and for the 18–24 age group is at 95%.[32] The constant engagement with online platforms has never been more prevalent.

These statistics, although powerful in illustrating the volume of online misogynistic abuse, only offer a snapshot of the situation. What these statistics (from relatively small-scale studies) cannot accurately reflect is the impact that this has on women's participation online. Society is increasingly 'digital', and, as such, interactions that traditionally have occurred offline are now transferring online. However, despite its prevalence, online misogyny is marginalised, trivialised, and ultimately, played down as a 'women's problem'. Furthermore, the ramifications of online misogyny, both for the woman who is the subject of such attacks and for the broader society, are oversimplified and even dismissed with an overwhelmingly common perception that if women want to participate online, they need to 'man up' or otherwise remove themselves from the online, abusive, and misogynistic environment. Therefore, combatting online misogyny is essential to ensure the equality of participation in the public sphere – which, in turn, is one of the key components of a democratic society.

Given the rise in engagement with digital platforms, it is unsurprising that there has been a sharp increase in both engagement and sexism online – it is now both increasingly present and much more visible to a far broader demographic. Interestingly, this has not been reflected as sharply in reported crime figures until recently. There has been a 30%

30 Girlguiding, 'Girls' Attitudes Survey 2016' (*Girlguiding*, 2016) <www.girlguiding.org.uk/globalassets/docs-and-resources/research-and-campaigns/girls-attitudes-survey-2016.pdf> accessed 10 September 2018, 17–19.

31 Ofcom, *Communications Market Report* (*Ofcom*, 2 August 2018) <www.ofcom.org.uk/research-and-data/multi-sector-research/cmr/cmr-2018/interactive> accessed 10 September 2018, 24.

32 ibid 26.

increase in stalking and harassment offences[33] in statistical reports from 2017 and 2018 respectively, which indicates that there is a growing trend for such behaviours but also that there is beginning to be some form of response, even if that is currently only realistically reflected in enhanced reporting figures. Irrespective of the minutiae in the detail of statistics, the broader message from all of these reports is that digital interactions are increasing in number and volume. Twitter alone records online activity in the region of 275 million[34] users per day, all of whom have the potential to send up to 2400 tweets per day.[35] If only a small percentage of all tweets are misogynistic and abusive, that is still a significant number. The statistics are shocking in terms of the prevalence of abuse online – approximately 40% of people have at some point experienced online abuse – albeit not purely misogynistic abuse – while 60% of Internet users have witnessed inappropriate or harmful content online.[36] More concerningly, despite the growth in this area, the resulting recognition of the problems associated with these online actions has been slow – a point recognised by both HM Government and the CPS in their admissions that exposure to hate crime online – including violence against women online – is not recorded in official statistics.[37] Despite this – and action being rather slow – a cross-government group on online misogyny was established in 2016, to "map out current action and to understand opportunities for action across government."[38] Whilst this is undoubtedly a small shuffle towards progress, it is almost too late to have any real impetus. The impact of online misogynistic abuse – particularly in a text-based form – is significant and is far from something that should become normalised. Efforts to counter it – whilst welcome – must be sustained and committed – and must involve more than mapping out

33 Although these figures are not entirely accurate because the increase is partly attributable – at least in some statistics – to the police mis-recording stalking as harassment. ONS, 'Crime in England and Wales: Year Ending March 2018' (*Office for National Statistics*, 19 July 2018) <www.ons.gov.uk/peoplepopulationandcommunity/crimeandjustice/bulletins/crimeinenglandandwales/yearendingmarch2018> accessed 10 September 2018, ch 11. For a full discussion of such a distinction, see Chapter 3, 3.5. Stalking, and 3.6. Harassment.

34 Twitter, 'About Twitter limits' (*Twitter*, 2018) <https://help.twitter.com/en/rules-and-policies/twitter-limits> accessed 10 September 2018.

35 Statista, 'Number of Twitter Users Worldwide from 2014 to 2020' (*Statista*, 2018) <www.statista.com/statistics/303681/twitter-users-worldwide/> accessed 10 September 2018.

36 Department for Digital, Culture, Media & Sport, *Internet Safety Strategy* (Green Paper, 2017) 42.

37 ibid 48.

38 ibid 51.

opportunities for action. To suggest that there are 'opportunities' for action is, at best, non-committal and, as such, contributes further to the notion that misogyny – particularly online misogyny – is not being taken seriously by the government. Such an approach – particularly in the aftermath of the most recent general election and the associated abuse of female politicians,[39] including the horrific murder of MP Jo Cox, who was brutally stabbed and killed during the Brexit campaign in 2016 – is the equivalent of applying a plaster to a severed artery.

2.3.1 The normalisation of online abuse

The prevalence of online abuse that has manifested itself as online misogyny and been directed at women – particularly in cases concerning influential and high-profile female campaigners – has become increasingly widespread. The commonalities of such abusive behaviour in a digital context is in itself problematic, particularly where the legal system is not well-placed to deal adequately with the potential criminal behaviours that such online misogyny gives rise to.[40] However, the concerns surrounding online misogyny are greater than only the online elements – where the online misogynistic abuse is the norm, it quickly manifests itself in offline abuse too. Such abuse is increasingly spreading from the online context to the offline context, changing from verbal threats and digital harassment, to potential stalking and consistent harassment in the offline environments. This is not limited to specific high-profile victims but is increasingly common in 'street abuse' situations – prevalent in public spaces.[41] The lack of responses and discouragement given to online misogyny allows such behaviour to be increasingly readily accepted as 'normal' and even 'acceptable'. Where this is the situation, the implications become even greater for the victims of such behaviour. The lack of challenge means that there is a growing perception that there will be no consequences for online

39 Azmina Dhrodia, 'Unsocial Media: Tracking Twitter Abuse against Women MPs' (*Medium*, 3 September 2017) <https://medium.com/@AmnestyInsights/unsocial-media-tracking-twitter-abuse-against-women-mps-fc28aeca498a> accessed 10 September 2018.

40 See discussions relating to legislative provisions in Chapter 3.

41 Louise Mullany and Loretta Trickett, 'Misogyny Hate Crime Evaluation Report' (*Nottingham Women's Centre*, 9 July 2018) <www.nottinghamwomenscentre.com/wp-content/uploads/2018/07/Misogyny-Hate-Crime-Evaluation-Report-June-2018.pdf> accessed 10 September 2018; BBC News, 'Misogyny Hate Crime in Nottinghamshire Gives 'Shocking' Results' (*BBC News*, 9 July 2018) <www.bbc.co.uk/news/uk-england-nottinghamshire-44740362> accessed 10 September 2018.

misogynistic abuse – a misperception arguably encouraged by the Crown Prosecution Service in its stance concerning social media offences which stipulates that there will only very rarely be public interest in pursuing a prosecution.[42] Given the lack of interest in pursuing prosecutions for such offences, it seems difficult to reconcile such a stance when the numbers of women reporting harassment and abuse continue to increase. This in itself indicates that this is an escalating problem and one which is increasingly prevalent.

The divide between online and offline abuse is a concern which is beginning to gain the attention of other prominent women. Lucy Powell MP has called for action to be taken to prevent reoccurrences of the Jo Cox murder[43] – such an escalation, whilst at present an unprecedented incident, has set an example for others to potentially follow. This is a manifestation of violence against women, encouraged and stimulated online, and escalated in the offline with physical violence and real, non-digital consequences. Jo Cox paid the ultimate price for being a prominent woman, who campaigned publicly. That said, there is no justification for murder on the basis of campaigning and speaking out on contentious issues. Yet, stalking and harassment – particularly on social media – seem to occur in a violence against women context specifically against females expressing opinions – a phenomenon highlighted through the examples offered by Caroline Criado-Perez and Stella Creasy.

2.3.2 Political campaigning and the 'techlash'

Caroline Criado-Perez, a feminist campaigner, and Stella Creasy MP were both subjected to a sustained course of online abusive behaviour conducted on micro-blogging site Twitter in late 2013. Perpetrators John Nimmo and Isabella Sorley were active on Twitter during 2013 and as part of this, targeted their vitriol at Criado-Perez and Creasy. The reason for this abuse and harassment was the campaign started by Criado-Perez – supported, then endorsed by Creasy – to ensure that

42 See 'Public Interest Stage of the Code for Prosecutors' in CPS, 'Social Media - Guidelines on Prosecuting Cases Involving Communications Sent via Social Media' (*Crown Prosecution Service*, revised 21 August 2018) <www.cps.gov.uk/legal-guidance/social-media-guidelines-prosecuting-cases-involving-communications-sent-social-media> accessed 10 September 2018. For more discussion on this point, see Chapter 3.

43 BBC News, 'Manchester MP Lucy Powell: 'Online Hate Abuse Moving Offline'' (*BBC News*, 24 May 2018) <www.bbc.co.uk/news/uk-england-manchester-44236615> accessed 10 September 2018.

high-profile historical female figures appear on banknotes issued by the Bank of England. In July 2013, the defendants composed and sent multiple tweets from their respective Twitter accounts. These messages included threats of violence – including sexual violence – and were menacing, and grossly offensive. There were a number of such tweets sent to both victims across a sustained period. After repeated efforts by the victims, the police finally became involved and the subsequent investigation led to both Nimmo and Sorley receiving charges for offences under s127 of the Communications Act 2003. The specific offences related to misuse of a public electronic communications network.

The defendants both entered guilty pleas and were sentenced by Judge Riddle. In his sentencing remarks, significant emphasis was placed on the harms and the impact during this sustained period of harassment, suffered by both victims. The remarks also identified that the victims had to incur significant expense in making themselves 'as untrackable as possible', due to the nature of the threats made against them. This recognition also included the impact of the behaviour of the defendants – who at the time of sending the messages, were anonymous to their victims – a factor, which in the opinion of Judge Riddle, heightened the fear of the recipients.[44] This judicial recognition is significant because it indicates that there is an awareness of the shift from online abuse to offline behaviour which is influenced by online communications.

Whilst the remarks in this case are significant, and it should be applauded for being the first prosecution of Twitter trolls in England & Wales,[45] the prosecution was one which was limited only to communications misuse offences.[46] Furthermore, it was also limited because it concerned high-profile women and, therefore, the implications of the harassment and threats are much more visible. There was no prosecution pursued against either defendant on this occasion for the threats, harassment or stalking behaviours which were inflicted by them – again indicative of the lack of interest by the CPS in pursuing social media offences.[47] As such, the judgment here is, simultaneously, noteworthy and

44 Kim Barker and Olga Jurasz, 'Submission of Evidence on Online Violence Against Women to the UN Special Rapporteur on Violence Against Women, its Causes and Consequences, Dr Dubravka Šimonović' (*Open University*, November 2017) <http://oro.open.ac.uk/52611/> accessed 10 September 2018, 14.

45 Kim Barker, '*R* v *Nimmo and Sorley* [2014]' in Erika Rackley and Rosemary Auchmuty (eds), *Women's Legal Landmarks: Celebrating 100 Years of Women and Law in the UK and Ireland* (Hart Publishing, 2018).

46 Communications Act 2003, s 127. For a fuller discussion of s127, see Chapter 3, 3.7 Communications networks.

47 See 'Public Interest Stage of the Code for Prosecutors' in CPS, 'Social Media - Guidelines on Prosecuting Cases Involving Communications Sent via Social Media'

disappointing. It does however have a lasting legacy, not simply because it is a 'first' but because it has identified the consequences of behaviours which transfer from the digital medium to the offline realm. This is a significant recognition for social media harms, specifically because it has taken so long for a judicial decision to reach this point. The case in itself – despite the custodial sentences – is however a disappointment, both for the lack of consideration of other, more substantive criminal offences, as well as for the lack of deterrence the custodial sentences had on the defendants. Within a matter of months, the defendants were back in court, facing further prosecutions for yet more Twitter abuse[48] – therefore, whilst online misogyny and online violence against women is spreading, the current stance taken by the justice system is one that is, arguably, insufficient to produce an appropriate response.

2.3.3 Intersectional abuse – still misogyny, still a 'techlash'?

Sadly the weaknesses in *Nimmo and Sorley* have become evident in other examples of social media cases, notably in *R v Viscount St Davids*.[49] High-profile Brexit remainer, Gina Miller, challenged the UK Government Brexit approach in the English courts shortly after the result of the referendum on leaving the European Union was announced. This legal challenge – again relating to a point of political campaigning – led to a significant and sustained level of online abuse targeting Miller. The defendant, Viscount St Davids – one of a number of online abusers – posted menacing content relating to Miller on Facebook. These posts included publicly putting a £5000 bounty on Miller. His first post on Facebook stated:

> £5,000 for the first person to 'accidentally' run over this bloody troublesome first-generation immigrant. This fucking boat jumper comes to our country, then believes she knows better than the people of our country, what is best for us. If this what we should expect from immigrants, send them back to their stinking jungles.

(*Crown Prosecution Service*, revised 21 August 2018) <www.cps.gov.uk/legal-guidance/social-media-guidelines-prosecuting-cases-involving-communications-sent-social-media> accessed 10 September 2018.

48 Jack Sommers, 'Troll John Nimmo Faces Second Prison Term for Tweeting Abuse to MP Luciana Berger' (*Huffington Post*, 27 June 2016) <www.huffingtonpost.co.uk/entry/twitter-troll-john-nimmo-faces-second-prison-term-for-tweeting-abuse-to-mp-luciana-berger_uk_5798d9cde4b0796a0b6139f5?guccounter=1> accessed 10 September 2018.

49 (n 3).

When the prosecution was raised, the court found that the defendant was fully aware of the menace contained within his posts on social media and he had intended that his posts were made up of such content. He was also found to have known that once the posts were written, they would be shared repeatedly by other Facebook users, spreading the menace and the level of threat.

The court found St Davids guilty of two of the three offences he was charged with under s127 Communications Act, with a further finding that the first charge relating to the comments about 'stinking jungles' was racially aggravated. The sentence handed down was for a custodial period of eight weeks. This was for the communications misuse offences and was increased to 12 weeks because of the racial aggravation present.

While the sentencing for the misuse of a different public electronic communications network – Facebook in this instance, rather than Twitter – is important because it indicates that prosecutions can – and will – be pursued across multiple platforms, it is also significant because it indicates that there is a greater willingness to address problems that are believed to be racially aggravated. The point here is that the aggravation for the offence was specifically commented on alongside the grossly offensive, and threatening character of the Facebook posts. Judge Arbuthnot commented in her sentencing remarks that the public profile of the victim was irrelevant when considering the nature of the impact upon her – a point that is somewhat recognisant of the position adopted in *Nimmo & Sorley*, albeit in that case specific attention was focussed on the level of abuse and the resulting safety measures deemed necessary by the victims because of their profiles. More significantly, judicial attention was again specifically paid to the need for Miller to engage additional personal security in the aftermath of the threats to her personal safety made by Viscount St Davids. The judge in the case also indicated that there was extreme racial abuse here – a point that is not specifically connected to the gender of the victim. As such, whilst this case is a significant step forward in terms of judicial involvement in social media prosecutions – especially in following similar reasoning in *Nimmo & Sorley* – it is also important to note that it deals with abuse beyond that generated by a hatred of women. The abuse here was exacerbated by the victim's gender *and* by her race – intersectional abuse which involves abuse of women because they are women is still behaviour which ought to fall within that contemplated as reprehensible by Lord Mackay in 1997.[50]

50 HL Deb 24 January 1997, vol 577, col 918 (Lord Chancellor, Lord Mackay of Clashfern)

2.4 Conclusion

The explosion in engagement and use of social media is responsible – at least in part – for an increase in reported social media abuse. The examples offered in this chapter are high-profile and unusual – specifically because both examples feature instances where prosecutions have been pursued – but of immense value nonetheless.

The examples of Criado-Perez, Creasy, and Miller arose as test-cases in the judicial system specifically because they involved harassment and abuse of high-profile women involved in high-profile campaigns. The prosecutions occurred because of their status in society and the media but in sentencing, the courts were pained to highlight that prosecutions and harm for online misogynistic abuse arise irrespective of the profile of the victim – a contradiction in terms. The harms inflicted on victims – especially those without public profiles should not be dismissed as trivial. Judge Arbuthnot in *Viscount St Davids* highlighted that regardless of public profile, no victim deserves to be the recipient of 'warped behaviour' – therefore whilst public figures may often be subjected to text-based abuses, they remain unjustifiable. Currently, prosecution numbers remain restricted – to date – to high-profile cases, because there is a lack of effective means of redress for victims:

> [i]n short, the key point here is that the profile of the alleged victim should be entirely irrelevant in terms of the alleged abuse received – the harm and the impact of the harm should be the determining features in tackling issues of online abuse.[51]

Problems surrounding misogynistic behaviours and prejudices are spreading from online media to offline actions, encouraging misperceptions concerning immunity for online actions. These misperceptions are encouraged by the lack of willingness to challenge existing systemic inequalities and embedded misperceptions surrounding misogyny more broadly within society. That said, there remain misunderstandings surrounding misogyny and especially online misogyny manifested as violence against women and girls. These misperceptions are not helped by the unwillingness to deal with socially-rooted misogynistic attitudes. Such trepidations are significant contributors to the narrow view of social media abuse as 'only bullying' or a factor in domestic abuse incidents. Whilst bullying and domestic violence

51 Barker and Jurasz, 'Submission of Evidence on Online Violence Against Women to the UN Special Rapporteur on Violence Against Women' (n 44) 15.

may involve instances of misogyny and of online abuse, online misogynistic abuse is broader than that and, as such, requires consideration from a much wider demographic. A multi-stakeholder approach is required to tackle the crippling misperceptions in this area.

There is a long and well-established history of feminist activism. It is time now for feminism to accept the latest challenge and step up to tackle this pernicious phenomenon head-on – it is not something that law or society alone can tackle effectively, particularly as there are gaps in the legislative landscape – the topic of discussion in the next chapter.

Bibliography

Table of cases

Chambers v DPP [2012] EWHC 2157 (Admin)
DPP v Collins [2006] UKHL 40
McAlpine v Bercow [2013] EWHC 1342 (QB)
R v Nimmo and Sorley (Westminster Magistrates' Court, 24 January 2014)
R v Viscount St Davids (Westminster Magistrates' Court, 11 July 2017)

Table of legislation and regulations

UK Public General Acts
Banking Act 2009
Communications Act 2003
Consumer Rights Act 2015
Criminal Justice and Courts Act 2015

EU Regulations
Regulation (EU) 2016/679 of the European Parliament and of the Council of 27 April 2016 on the protection of natural persons with regard to the processing of personal data and on the free movement of such data, and repealing Directive 95/46/EC (General Data Protection Regulation) (GDPR)

List of secondary sources

Books
Jane EA, *Misogyny Online: A Short (and Brutish) History* (SAGE 2017)
Golding D and van Deventer L, *Game Changers: From Minecraft to Misogyny, the Fight for the Future of Videogames* (Affirm Press 2016)
Ryan J, *A History of the Internet and the Digital Future* (Reaktion Books 2010)

Command Papers
Department for Digital, Culture, Media & Sport, *Internet Safety Strategy* (Green Paper, 2017)

Contributions to Edited Books

Barker K, '*R v Nimmo and Sorley* [2014]' in Rackley E and Auchmuty R (eds), *Women's Legal Landmarks: Celebrating 100 Years of Women and Law in the UK and Ireland* (Hart Publishing, 2018)

Crown Prosecution Service Guidelines

CPS, 'Social Media – Guidelines on Prosecuting Cases Involving Communications Sent via Social Media' (*Crown Prosecution Service*, revised 21 August 2018) <www.cps.gov.uk/legal-guidance/social-media-guidelines-prosecuting-cases-involving-communications-sent-social-media> accessed 10 September 2018

European Commission Documents

Commission, 'Proposal for a Directive of the European Parliament and of the Council on Combating Fraud and Counterfeiting of Non-Cash Means of Payment and Replacing Council Framework Decision 2001/413/JHA' COM (2017) 489 final

Evidence Submissions

Barker K and Jurasz O, 'Submission of Evidence on Online Violence Against Women to the UN Special Rapporteur on Violence Against Women, its Causes and Consequences, Dr Dubravka Šimonović' (*Open University*, November 2017) <http://oro.open.ac.uk/52611/> accessed 10 September 2018

Hansard Reports

HL Deb 24 January 1997, vol 577, col 918

IGO Publications

Gagliardone I and others, *Countering Online Hate Speech* (UNESCO 2015) <http://unesdoc.unesco.org/images/0023/002332/233231e.pdf> accessed 10 September 2018

Newspaper Articles

Bates L, 'Sexism in Schools is Real – How Can the Department for Education Deny It?' *The Guardian* (London, 31 March 2016) <https://www.theguardian.com/commentisfree/2016/mar/31/sexism-schools-department-of-education-deny-sexist-bullying> accessed 10 September 2018

Bowcott O, 'Social Media Firms Must Face Heavy Fines over Extremist Content – MPs' *The Guardian* (London, 1 May 2017) <www.theguardian.com/media/2017/may/01/social-media-firms-should-be-fined-for-extremist-content-say-mps-google-youtube-facebook> accessed 10 September 2018

Flood R, 'Users Fear Social Media is Making Them Ill, but They Still Can't Stop' *The Independent* (London, 26 February 2017) <www.independent.co.uk/news/world/americas/smartphone-social-media-apps-mental-health-

negative-check-plugged-in-communication-technology-a7600686.html> accessed 10 September 2018

Matharu H, 'Reclaim the Internet Campaign to Tackle 'Colossal' Scale of Online Misogyny' *The Independent* (London, 26 May 2016) <www.independent.co.uk/news/uk/home-news/research-reveals-colossal-scale-of-online-misogyny-a7049396.html> accessed 10 September 2018

Rawlinson K, 'Toby Young Faces Fresh Calls for his Sacking in Misogyny Row' *The Guardian* (London, 7 January 2018) <www.theguardian.com/media/2018/jan/07/toby-young-faces-fresh-calls-for-his-sacking-in-misogyny-row> accessed 10 September 2018.

Parliamentary Reports

Communications Select Committee, *Social Media and Criminal Offences* (HL 2014–15, 37)

Home Affairs Committee, *Hate Crime: Abuse, Hate and Extremism Online* (HC 2016–17, 609)

Reports

APA, 'Stress in America: Coping with Change' (10th edn, *American Psychological Association* 2017) <www.apa.org/news/press/releases/stress/2016/coping-with-change.PDF> accessed 10 September 2018

Baran P, 'On a Distributed Command and Control System Configuration' (*RAND*, 31 December 1960) <www.rand.org/content/dam/rand/pubs/research_memoranda/2009/RM2632.pdf> accessed 10 September 2018

Demos, 'The Use of Misogynistic Terms on Twitter' (*Demos*, 2016) <www.demos.co.uk/wp-content/uploads/2016/05/Misogyny-online.pdf> accessed 10 September 2018

Girlguiding, 'Girls' Attitudes Survey 2016' (*Girlguiding*, 2016) <www.girlguiding.org.uk/globalassets/docs-and-resources/research-and-campaigns/girls-attitudes-survey-2016.pdf> accessed 10 September 2018

Mullany L and Trickett L, 'Misogyny Hate Crime Evaluation Report' (*Nottingham Women's Centre*, 9 July 2018) <www.nottinghamwomenscentre.com/wp-content/uploads/2018/07/Misogyny-Hate-Crime-Evaluation-Report-June-2018.pdf> accessed 10 September 2018

Ofcom, 'Communications Market Report' (*Ofcom*, 2 August 2018) <www.ofcom.org.uk/research-and-data/multi-sector-research/cmr/cmr-2018/interactive> accessed 10 September 2018

ONS, 'Crime in England and Wales: Year Ending March 2018' (*Office for National Statistics*, 19 July 2018) <www.ons.gov.uk/peoplepopulationandcommunity/crimeandjustice/bulletins/crimeinenglandandwales/yearendingmarch2018> accessed 10 September 2018

Websites

Amnesty International, 'Amnesty Reveals Alarming Impact of Online Abuse against Women' (*Amnesty International*, 20 November 2017) <www.amnesty.org/en/latest/news/2017/11/amnesty-reveals-alarming-impact-of-online-abuse-against-women/> accessed 10 September 2018

BBC News, 'Manchester MP Lucy Powell: 'Online Hate Abuse Moving Offline'' (*BBC News*, 24 May 2018) <www.bbc.co.uk/news/uk-england-manchester-44236615> accessed 10 September 2018

BBC News, 'Misogyny Hate Crime in Nottinghamshire Gives 'Shocking' Results' (*BBC News*, 9 July 2018) <www.bbc.co.uk/news/uk-england-nottinghamshire-44740362> accessed 10 September 2018

BBC News, 'Stalking reports treble as prosecution rates fall' (*BBC News*, 20 July 2018) <www.bbc.co.uk/news/uk-england-44887574> accessed 10 September 2018

Dhrodia A, 'Unsocial Media: Tracking Twitter Abuse against Women MPs' (*Medium*, 3 September 2017) <https://medium.com/@AmnestyInsights/unsocial-media-tracking-twitter-abuse-against-women-mps-fc28aeca498a> accessed 10 September 2018

Hess A, 'Why Women Aren't Welcome on the Internet' (*Pacific Standard*, 6 January 2014) <https://psmag.com/social-justice/women-arent-welcome-internet-72170> accessed 10 September 2018

Nandra JS, 'The Dark Side of Gaming: "I've Been Called a Curry Muncher…"' (*BBC Three*, 7 March 2018) <https://www.bbc.co.uk/bbcthree/article/9fe76f89-2d48-4393-bbdd-d6b15b0b0503> accessed 10 September 2018

RSPH, 'RSPH Announces 'Scroll Free September' Campaign to Improve Mental Health and Wellbeing' (*Royal Society for Public Health*, 27 July 2018) <www.rsph.org.uk/about-us/news/rsph-announces-scroll-free-september-campaign-to-improve-mental-health-and-wellbeing.html> accessed 10 September 2018

Sommers J, 'Troll John Nimmo Faces Second Prison Term for Tweeting Abuse to MP Luciana Berger' (*Huffington Post*, 27 June 2016) <www.huffingtonpost.co.uk/entry/twitter-troll-john-nimmo-faces-second-prison-term-for-tweeting-abuse-to-mp-luciana-berger_uk_5798d9cde4b0796a0b6139f5?guccounter=1> accessed 10 September 2018

Statista, 'Number of Twitter Users Worldwide from 2014 to 2020' (*Statista*, 2018) <www.statista.com/statistics/303681/twitter-users-worldwide/> accessed 10 September 2018

Twitter, 'About Twitter limits' (*Twitter*, 2018) <https://help.twitter.com/en/rules-and-policies/twitter-limits> accessed 10 September 2018

3 Online communications

The legal landscape

> We consider that the current range of offences, notably those found in the Protection from Harassment Act 1997, is sufficient to prosecute bullying conducted using social media. Similarly, sending a communication which is grossly offensive and has the purpose of causing distress or anxiety is an offence under section 1 of the Malicious Communications Act 1988. Although we understand that "trolling" causes offence, we do not see a need to create a specific and more severely punished offence for this behaviour.
>
> House of Lords Communications Select Committee, 2015.[1]

3.1 Introduction – comprehension, competence, and cohesion?

The phenomenon of online misogyny is one which poses – and continues to pose – challenges for the legal system. Given the current regulatory problems which are posed by this social phenomenon, suggestions for legal reforms are worthy of consideration, not least because of the harms which are caused by such behaviours. These harms are rarely recognised by the reactive legal system. It must be stated however that legal changes alone will not be solutions to this problem but offer one element of a strategy to deal with online misogyny. The problem, as has been set out earlier in this book,[2] is one which is multi-faceted and, as such, singular one-dimensional solutions would be highly unlikely to succeed.

There has been an overwhelming failure by the legal system to recognise the pernicious harms and impacts caused by online misogyny,

1 Communications Select Committee, *Social Media and Criminal Offences* (HL 2014 – 15, 37).

2 See, for example, discussions in Chapter 1 – 1.3. Addressing online misogyny through law: the limitations.

DOI: 10.4324/9780429956805-3

and this failure is compounded by the parallel failings of technology companies and social media platforms. The legal system has reinforced this failure by failing to hold those companies and platforms to account for their role in the facilitation of such abusive behaviours by the users of such platforms.

These failures are presented here as multi-faceted and stem from a wide-spread social demographic problem. Yet, whilst these are significant, they are not solely responsible for the phenomenon under discussion. The rise and prominence of these problems is also attributable – at least in part – to the rise in the ease of access to portable devices and online platforms.[3] However, more than that, all of this has led to a change in accepted social norms which means that the development in technologies have spurred a displacement in social attitudes where it is seemingly acceptable to be abusive online, even where that behaviour is not necessarily mirrored offline.[4] This is not a problem which falls to be addressed solely by the legal system. However, the legal system must recognise the phenomenon and be prepared to tackle it – something which thus far has not happened despite other related forms of online abuse being addressed legislatively. Therefore, the discussion in this chapter outlines the current legislative problems *because* the legal system is least well placed to tackle this issue. The phenomenon of online misogynistic abuse is one which is systematic and reflective of a patriarchal society, rife with structural inequalities. Nevertheless, the legal recognition of such a problem and the harm it causes would be a high-profile indicator that these behaviours are no longer acceptable, and that it is no longer 'cool' to be a troll.

Furthermore, whilst an assessment of the legal provisions dealing with online misogyny, and online violence against women more broadly, suggests that there is a plethora of potential legal provisions which *could* apply to this issue, these are currently underutilised or unsuitable. This chapter will, therefore, outline the current legal landscape, highlighting the lacuna which exists in relation to online misogyny and text-based abuse behaviours presenting a compelling argument for *better*, rather than more, legal regulation.[5] Appropriate

3 For more on this point, see Chapter 2 – 2.3.1. *The Normalisation of Online Abuse.*

4 Kim Barker and Olga Jurasz, 'Gender, Human Rights and Cybercrime: Are Virtual Worlds Really That Different?' in Michael Asimow, Kathryn Brown and David Ray Papke (eds), *Law and Popular Culture: International Perspectives* (Cambridge Scholars Publishing 2014) 87.

5 That said, it must be noted that whilst the discussion here focuses on the legal provisions relating to the UK, and England, and Scotland, there are legislative limitations imposed on both Scotland, by virtue of devolution, and the UK, by virtue of its – at the time of writing – membership of the European Union. Limitations

and proportional regulation is required, but so too is enforcement. It is all very well having *better* legal provisions but if enforcement and prosecution continue to be poor, only a partial solution can be offered from the legal system, and even then, it is redress rather than a solution. The current legal landscape is one which lacks comprehensive, appropriate provisions for dealing with social media abuse. Beyond that, it also lacks cohesion, suggesting that there is a disconnect between the social phenomenon and the justice system in this area.

3.2 The limitation paradox

As with any area of law, there are a number of overlapping areas and, indeed, a number of conflicting priorities. This is true of online misogyny, especially in the sphere of communications law. There are a number of legal provisions which could be applied to the issue of online text-based abuse. That said, the situation is complex; while provisions *could* be applied, the standard for prosecution is currently recognised as being too high.[6] This alone is one facet but it is not the sole factor on which responsibility rests. To suggest so would be a gross oversimplification of the legal landscape and the competing demands made of it. The authors suggest here that the answer to tackling this phenomenon is *not* necessarily more legislation but *better* legislation, and *better use* of existing legislation to ensure that the issue is addressed comprehensively, competently, and cohesively.

---

also exist in the enforcement of potentially relevant provisions by evidence collation issues, alongside jurisdictional concerns – particularly pressing in light of the so-called "borderless" Internet. This volume does not discuss issues relating to conflicts of law, or Internet regulation broadly conceived, but see: Directive 2000/31/EC of the European Parliament and of the Council of 8 June 2000 on Certain Legal Aspects of Information Society Services, in Particular Electronic Commerce, in the Internal Market ('Directive on Electronic Commerce') [2000] OJ L178/1, art 12 (hereafter, e-Commerce Directive 2000); *R v Sheppard* [2010] EWCA Crim 65, [2010] 1 WLR 2779; *Delfi AS v Estonia* App no 64569/09 (ECtHR, 16 June 2015).

6 Council of Europe Parliamentary Assembly Committee on Equality and Non-Discrimination, 'Ending Cyberdiscrimination and Online Hate, Report by Rapporteur Marit Maij' (13 December 2016) Doc 14217 <http://semantic-pace.net/tools/pdf.aspx?doc=aHR0cDovL2Fzc2VtYmx5LmNvZS5pbnQvbncveG1sL-1hSZWYvWDJILURXLWV4dHIuYXNwP2ZpbGVpZD0yMzIzNCZsYW5n-PUVO&xsl=aHR0cDovL3NlbWFudGljcGFjZS5uZXQvWHNsdC9QZGYvW-FJlZi1XRC1BVC1YTUwyUERGLnhzbA==&xsltparams=ZmlsZW1kPTIz-MjM0> accessed 10 September 2018, para 32.

3.2.1 The Devolution settlement

To such an end, the legislative landscape and legal structures within the UK present one of the first hurdles to tackling this challenge. Whilst many of the communications provisions operate within either Scotland or England & Wales respectively, very few provisions are UK-wide. In this context, Scotland adopts different approaches compared to England & Wales, with the European level contributing to an additional, third layer of differentiation. At present the UK must comply with EU legal provisions – and therefore some of the legal provisions in this area are restricted to the competence of the Westminster Government under the devolution settlement. This will, in turn, have implications for the timeliness and quality of the legal responses. For instance, Scotland, whilst more progressive in its outlook, has one hand tied behind its back in attempting to tackle online text-based abuse and online misogyny. This is especially the situation because of the reserved competences Westminster holds in respect of communications law – the provisions within the Communications Act 2003 are – unusually – some of those which apply across the UK. Scotland therefore, is unable to legislate to alter these provisions as to do so would be *ultra vires.*[7] Consequently, the statutory provision which is – under current law – arguably most suited to dealing with issues of abusive communications, cannot be amended by the Scottish Government. This is therefore a fairly significant limitation in the context of legislative competence, and irrespective of the focus or desire of the Scottish Government to tackle this issue, it is unable to alter this provision. Ultimately, legal provisions in Scotland have had to accommodate it and supplement it.

3.2.2 The European Union remit

The other limitation which is relevant in the context of the legal landscape is that of the overarching EU legal provisions. Whilst these are not the same as the provisions in operation domestically, the provisions at an EU level make the regulatory sphere somewhat more complicated in terms of attributing responsibility and regulating this sphere. Notably, the e-Commerce Directive[8] operates to ensure that there is a liability shield for platform providers and Internet intermediaries. In short, these provisions mean that Twitter, Facebook,

7 Scotland Act 1998, s 29(4).
8 e-Commerce Directive 2000, art 12.

YouTube, and other 'Internet Giants' cannot be held liable for content posted on their platforms. This shield was designed to operate in the context of intellectual property infringements in light of the advent of illegal downloads and streaming, but has – as one of its unintended consequences – meant that the same shield applies in the context of hate speech, online text-based abuses, and other potential criminality perpetrated through social media sites. These provisions cannot be changed at a domestic level – in this regard, both the Scottish Government and the Westminster Government have to live with these limitations. Unfortunately, so too do the victims of online text-based abuses and online misogyny. This is a serious limitation, compounded by the fact that the very same Directive imposes no monitoring obligation[9] on the Internet Giants. Not only are they not responsible for the content posted on and shared through their platforms, but they are also under no legal obligation to monitor their sites for illegal content, a further – and more harmful – limitation on the methods of redress victims could have.[10]

3.2.3 Limitations – competence v cohesion?

Given the limitations discussed here in the ability of the legislatures to change legal provisions in this area, it is difficult to envisage any cohesion in tackling the phenomenon of online misogyny. This in itself is frustrating because the very system which *could* signpost change is the one which is *reluctant* to recognise the problem. The limitations add a further layer of complexity if the phenomenon is considered as a multi-faceted problem. It *is* such a problem, but unfortunately most attention paid to it has, to date, focussed on singular – and often different – perspectives, such as image-based sexual abuse.

The predominant consideration is one of a free speech perspective, and the claims are that it is impossible to regulate this area because of free speech entitlements.[11] These arguments will not be

9 ibid, art 15.

10 Although this could arguably be about to change in light of the discussions that social media platforms and Internet Giants have been having with the European Commission. Aside from those discussions, the recent Recommendation on Illegal Content Online suggests that changes are envisaged at a European level on the monitoring point: Commission, 'European Commission and IT Companies Announce Code of Conduct on Illegal Online Hate Speech' (Press Release, Brussels, 31 May 2016) <http://europa.eu/rapid/press-release_IP-16-1937_en.htm> accessed 10 September 2018.

11 See below for discussions on limitations to freedom of expression at 3.7. Communications networks and Chapter 4 – 4.2.2. *Hate crime v Hate speech*.

repeated here – from the perspective of communications law, there are two significant limitations on the ability to address this issue – that does not however mean that it should be ignored, nor should it be brushed aside. This is a pressing problem – and one which the various legal jurisdictions have skirted around, despite the evidence suggesting that this is a hugely pressing social issue.[12] Nowhere is the issue of women's safety more prominently a feature of policy than in Scotland.

3.3 Legal challenges of online communications – where does the problem lie?

None of online abuse, online misogyny, or online text-based abuse appear in the legal system as criminal offences, nor are they listed as misuse of communications network offences. These activities are not listed in statutory provisions, nor are they common law offences within the UK nor its jurisdictions of England & Wales, nor Scotland.[13] Similarly, there is no legal provision dealing with social media text-based abuse, nor online harassment. All of these – as behaviours specific to the digital age – have emerged fairly recently, particularly as a result of the shift in Internet usage from Web 1.0 to Web 2.0, with Internet users increasingly contributing to the development of Internet content through posting on platforms such as social media. Consequently, this has led to new behaviours emerging that the legal system and predated legislation could not have envisaged at the time of drafting, nor enactment. In some respects, therefore, legislation dealing with communications issues should be heralded for its longevity. That said, when it comes to dealing with issues of online abuse, the legislation is no longer being utilised effectively and has reached its watershed moment. The legal provisions addressing communications regulation require updating, and, with a particular focus on gender-based harms and abuses, the statute book more broadly needs to become reflective of the behaviours witnessed in society now.

Not only does the legal system overwhelmingly fail to recognise non-traditional harms and non-traditional gender-based abuses, it also fails to recognise emerging forms of abusive behaviour, such

12 For statistics representing this phenomenon, see discussions in Chapter 2.

13 Northern Ireland is not considered within this work. Discussions therefore focus on the UK, and England & Wales, as legal jurisdictions with occasional specific examples from Scotland.

as those committed purely in a digital space. This is increasingly apparent, despite indicators suggesting that this issue will continue to be one which is prevalent in a progressively digital society.[14] In the last five years in the UK, attention has gradually begun to focus on highlighting these behaviours – but in that time, the legal responses have been incredibly limited. The abuse directed towards high-profile women politicians,[15] alongside high-profile women celebrities,[16] and high-profile outspoken women[17] has added weight to the calls for reform in this area. Initiatives by politicians[18] and campaign groups have also attracted some attention[19] – but in a manner resembling that of a passing fad, rather than a movement for lasting change with a real impact. That said, the law has not yet responded to such calls – misperceptions continue to exist and only small – but significant – steps have been taken to address partial aspects of this broader phenomenon. Notably, the introduction of new criminal offences dealing with revenge pornography,[20] or image-based sexual abuse,[21] through legislative amendments which tackle some elements of online abuse, only focuses specifically on one form of activity involving images taken and shared illicitly. That said, these are the limited instances by which the legal system

14 For example, concerns are growing about the potential for smart-homes to become instruments of coercion and control. Brian H Spitzberg and William R Cupach, 'The State of the Art of Stalking: Taking Stock of the Emerging Literature' (2007) 12 Aggression and Violent Behaviour 64; Roxanne Leitão, 'When Smart Homes Become Smart Prisons' (*DigiCult*) <https://digicult.it/news/when-smart-homes-become-smart-prisons/#_edn1> accessed 10 September 2018; Phoebe Braithwaite, 'Smart Home Tech Is Being Turned into a Tool for Domestic Abuse' (*Wired*, 22 July 2018) <www.wired.co.uk/article/internet-of-things-smart-home-domestic-abuse> accessed 10 September 2018.

15 Amnesty International, 'Toxic Twitter – A Toxic Place for Women' (*Amnesty International*,2018)<www.amnesty.org/en/latest/research/2018/03/online-violence-against-women-chapter-1/> accessed 10 September 2018.

16 *R v Nimmo and Sorley* (Westminster Magistrates' Court, 24 January 2014).

17 *R v Viscount St Davids* (Westminster Magistrates' Court, 11 July 2017).

18 Yvette Cooper, 'Why I'm Campaigning to Reclaim the Internet from Sexist Trolls' *The Telegraph* (London, 26 May 2016) <www.telegraph.co.uk/women/politics/why-im-campaigning-to-reclaim-the-internet-from-sexist-trolls/> accessed 10 September 2018.

19 See, for example, Glitch!UK <https://seyiakiwowo.com/GlitchUK/> accessed 10 September 2018; Reclaim the Internet <http://www.reclaimtheinternet.com> accessed 10 September 2018.

20 Criminal Justice and Courts Act 2015, ss 32 – 35. Hereafter, CJCA 2015.

21 Clare McGlynn and Erika Rackley, 'Image-Based Sexual Abuse' (2017) 37 OJLS 534.

includes provisions dealing with 'abuse'.[22] Therefore, the discussions within this chapter focus on social media abuse in the form of textual messages – to that end, *none* of the existing legal provisions categorise such behaviours under the heading of 'abuse.' Whilst the introduction of provisions to deal with this is welcome, it should not be mistakenly interpreted as a comprehensive solution. As it stands, these provisions would be too one-dimensional, and overlook a number of other forms of online abuse that are unregulated, including text-based abuses.[23]

The traditional argument advanced – and one cited most often – in response to suggestions of regulating social media platforms and social media posts is that to do so would infringe upon freedom of expression rights under the European Convention on Human Rights.[24] This is a position which suggests there is an absolute freedom to say what one wishes in any medium, irrespective of the harm or potential criminality of the act. Such a position fails to acknowledge that there can be consequences for expressions which are harmful, or potentially criminal.[25] Whilst freedom of expression is also a factor in the discussions about regulating online communications, it is not a 'get out of jail free card' for online text-based abuses, primarily because the right to freedom of expression is not one which goes unchecked and, as such, proportionate and necessary limitations[26] can be imposed on it.[27] Equally, there are occasions where there *ought* to be consequences where speech which, whilst freely expressed, causes significant harm.

The current legal landscape in the UK – at least in respect of communications provisions – does not fully address the consequences of harmful, or hateful speech, even where there is recognisable

22 The discussions in this volume – and in this chapter – are not concerned with domestic abuse, or child-sexual abuse. That is not to say that online social-media abuse is not related to these other areas, simply that the discussions here have a different focus.

23 The discussions within this chapter focus on non-image-based abuses, referred to as text-based abuses.

24 Convention for the Protection of Human Rights and Fundamental Freedoms (European Convention on Human Rights, as amended) (ECHR).

25 Kim Barker and Olga Jurasz, 'Submission of Evidence to Scottish Government Independent Review of Hate Crime Legislation (Bracadale Review)' (*Open University*, December 2017) <http://oro.open.ac.uk/52612/> accessed 10 September 2018, 10.

26 ECHR, art 8(2).

27 See below for discussions on limitations to freedom of expression at 3.7. Communications networks and Chapter 4 at – 4.2.2. *Hate crime v Hate speech*.

harm.[28] The relevant legal provisions – which are discussed below – are inadequate in, and ineffective for, addressing online text-based abuses. In particular, those leading to gender-based harms which manifest themselves as forms of online violence against women. Part of this inevitable difficulty is that there are a number of behaviours that the legal system recognises as being harmful to society – including stalking, harassment, and abuse – into which social media abuse and online text-based abuses could fall. That said, the provisions dealing with stalking, harassment, and abuse neglect to provide adequate and proportional mechanisms for dealing with social media abuses, especially where those behaviours include abuse which is gender-based.[29]

These factors all combine to make for a congested and imperfect legal situation. Currently, the legal provisions which could be applicable to instances of online text-based abuses span criminal provisions encompassing threats, criminal provisions dealing with harassing and stalking behaviours, communications network misuse offences, and potentially, hate crime provisions. All of these combined mean that the legislative provisions offer a number of *potential* routes of recourse – yet the reality of the situation is far from clear-cut. As such, the following discussions consider the problems posed by online text-based abuses, sent through social media platforms, under each of these respective categories of legislative provision.

Behaviours which include the making of threats – either to kill, or inflict sexual violence are dealt with in Chapter 3 – Part I. Behaviours which give rise to complaints of stalking or harassment are then addressed in discussions falling within Chapter 3 – Part II, whilst the less substantive, but still criminal, offences dealing with misuse of a public electronic communications network are addressed in Chapter 3 – Part III. Finally, where criminal acts conducted through online text-based abuses on social media are motivated through hatred, and in particular the hatred of women, the legal responses to such bias are considered in Chapter 4.

28 The authors do not suggest that freedom of expression *ought* to be limited but recognise the fact that the existing provisions that – on paper at least – could address the consequences of free expression rights in an online context are seldom used. See below at 3.7. Communications networks.

29 For more on discussions surrounding gender-based abuses, see the discussions in Chapter 1.

Part I

Threats and threats to kill

Many of those who have experienced online abuse have received abusive messages containing threats. In the most high-profile cases in this area, the threats made have included threats to rape, physically assault, or kill,[30] or any combination of all three. For instance, there was no prosecution case advanced in *R v Nimmo and Sorley* under the Offences Against the Person Act 1861,[31] which makes it an offence for a person to threaten to kill another if that other would believe the killing was to be carried out,[32] despite numerous messages threatening to kill being sent to victims. The messages, sent by the defendants, John Nimmo and Isabella Sorley, through social media platforms quite clearly fall within the scope of the s16 offence, yet were not prosecuted as such. The messages – including the threats to kill – from Sorley included:

> Fuck off and die (. . .) you should have jumped in front of horses, go die; I will find you and you don't want to know what I will do when I do (. . .) kill yourself before I do; rape is the last of your worries; I've just got out of prison and would happily do more time to see you berried; seriously go kill yourself! I will get less time for that; rape?! I'd do a lot worse things than rape you.[33]

Similar threatening and abusive messages were also sent by Nimmo, who was no different in his behaviour:[34]

> Ya not that gd looking to rape u be fine; I will find you; come to Geordie land bitch; just think it could be somebody that knows

30 *Nimmo and Sorley* (n 16); *Viscount St Davids* (n 17). See also Everyday Sexism Project <https://everydaysexism.com> accessed 10 September 2018.

31 Hereafter, OAPA 1861.

32 ibid, s 16.

33 *Nimmo and Sorley* (n 16) 2 (Riddle J), judgment accessible at <www.judiciary.uk/wp-content/uploads/JCO/Documents/Judgments/r-v-nimmo-and-sorley.pdf> accessed 10 September 2018.

34 Kim Barker, '*R* v *Nimmo and Sorley* [2014]' in Erika Rackley and Rosemary Auchmuty (eds), *Women's Legal Landmarks: Celebrating 100 Years of Women and Law in the UK and Ireland* (Hart Publishing, 2018) (forthcoming).

> you personally; the police will do nothing; rape her nice ass; could I help with that lol; the things I cud do to u; dumb blond bitch.[35]

Despite the seriousness of such threats, very few of the 'social media' cases have been challenged under criminal offences dealing with the making of threats to kill.

3.4 Threats and threats to kill

The OAPA s16 wording – introduced in 1977[36] – is intended to cover a much wider range of conduct than that envisaged in the original drafting from 1861; a point elucidated in the Court of Appeal in *R v Peter's (Juliet)*[37] where the conduct complained of consisted of the leaving of threatening messages on answer machines of a record company. The messages contained threats made against a well-known singer and, as such, the Court of Appeal had no hesitation in indicating that such threats fell squarely within the remit of the revised s16:

> We think that s16 as it is now drafted was simply drafted in a way to make it clear that any conduct of the kind suggested, however it came about, came within the provisions of the offence. It did not need to be by any letter or writing or restricted in any way like that, and we can see no justification at all for interpreting that section in a limited way and think it entirely right and proper to interpret it in the way that would cover the conduct (. . .).[38]

Given that threats made via an answering machine could fall within s16, it is difficult to understand why there have been very, very few prosecutions made when messages containing threats have been sent via social media. A potential application of s16 to such threats would also give this section a contemporary contextual interpretation – in a manner similar to that which the Court of Appeal adopted in *Peter's* over 15 years ago. This is a point which seems to have been largely overlooked despite the controversy surrounding the decision

35 *Nimmo and Sorley* (n 16) 2 (Riddle J), judgment accessible at <www.judiciary.uk/wp-content/uploads/JCO/Documents/Judgments/r-v-nimmo-and-sorley.pdf> accessed 10 September 2018.

36 Amended by the Criminal Law Act 1977, sch 12.

37 *R v Peter's* [2002] EWCA Crim 1721. Hereafter, *Peter's*.

38 ibid [32] (Kay LJ).

in *Chambers v DPP* [2012][39] to prosecute on the basis of a joke made via Twitter concerning the blowing up of an airport. Seemingly, the meaning of the words used in the threat is to be given due consideration and should be, "gathered from the vulgar import, and not from any technical legal sense."[40] The s16 offence requires that the person who makes the threat intends the other person to fear it will be carried out. That said, the courts have – in the aftermath of *Chambers* – made it very clear that where there is evidence of a joke, or that the person making the threat was not serious, then the situation could be different on the basis of a lack of intent. Whilst very few social media prosecutions have been pursued under s16 OAPA, it seems that the legacy of *Chambers* is not to be understated – a point highlighted recently by the High Court of England & Wales, which stipulated that the context in which the threat has been made is a vital consideration.[41] In the age of social media – given the new emphasis placed on the context in which the threat is made – it is even more difficult to see why there has been no enforcement, or prosecution action, taken against those who issue threats to harm, and kill, under this provision. This inaction appears short-sighted, especially as there is clear precedent for including within the s16 offence means of threat making which were not envisaged in the original drafting. If answer phone messages can be sufficient to give rise to a prosecution – and a successful one – for making threats, then so too should threatening messages sent via social media.

Similarly, alongside the OAPA, there is greater scope for prosecutions to be levied under various public order offences. Under such legislation, a number of offences include provisions designed to address threatening behaviours – albeit of a lesser level of seriousness than under the OAPA. For example, under the Public Order Act 1986,[42] several offences purport to deal with threatening, abusive, or harassing behaviours. It is possible that social media abuse, particularly threats made via social media platforms, could also fall within these provisions. Again, – much like the OAPA provisions – very few social media messages containing threats have been met with prosecutions pursued under the POA.

The current wording of the POA – amended in 2006 – makes it an offence to use threatening, abusive, or insulting words or behaviour,[43] or to display to another person any writing or visible representation

39 *Chambers v DPP* [2012] EWHC 2157 (Admin). Hereafter, *Chambers*.
40 *Colman v Godwin* (1783) 3 Doug KB 90, 91 (Buller J).
41 *Dhir v Saddler* [2017] EWHC 3155 QB.
42 Hereafter, POA 1986.
43 ibid, s 4(1).

which itself is threatening, abusive, or insulting[44] with the intention of causing the person to whom threats are made to believe that, "immediate unlawful violence will be used against him" or "to provoke the immediate use of unlawful violence by that person." The provision here is quite clear in that where threats are made to another person – either in person or in writing – that could be sufficient to satisfy s4. In the event of threats sent via a social media platform to another user of that platform, providing there is first, an intent and second, a belief that violence may be used, there is enough to form the basis of a s4 offence.

Judicial consideration makes it abundantly clear that the words 'used towards' that are contained within the s4(1)(a) offence connote the physical presence of the person against whom the words were used.[45] This is therefore a problem in terms of prosecuting social media threats, due to the lack of physical proximity of the person sending the threats and the person who is intended to receive them – the specific problem presented by online abuse and threats is the distance and separation between the parties.[46] It is an essential requirement of the s4(1)(a) offence that the words communicated from the person making the threat must be heard by the person to whom the threat is made. If a third party – such as a retweeter – makes the words known to the intended victim, this will not satisfy the elements of the offence. This is the essence of the problem in terms of prosecuting social media threats under s4 of the POA – there has to be an immediacy of violence or provocation of violence, and the threat must be heard by the person against whom it is made. As such, in instances where social media threats are sent purely electronically, it is unlikely that s4(1)(a) will be of use. It would nevertheless, be interesting to see judicial consideration of the 'distribution' / 'display' point in the context of social media threats being made.

Despite that, in *R (Hogle) v DPP* [2015][47] the Court stated that language used by a defendant, together with his behaviour, could be sufficient to satisfy the offence by causing real fear and distress, even if there is no specific finding of any intention to cause immediate unlawful violence. That said, it seems unlikely that there will be a departure from the requirement of physical presence from *Atkin,* and therefore s4 of the Public Order Act appears to be of limited use in tackling online threats. The threats contemplated by s4(1)(a) POA do not have

44 ibid, s 4(2)
45 *Atkin v DPP* [1989] Crim LR 581.
46 Yet this in many instances exacerbates the level of fear and alarm, and harm caused.
47 *R (Hogle) v DPP* [2015] ACD 84. Hereafter, *R (Hogle).*

to take the same form as the threats made under s16 OAPA, as the s4 offence requires threats of violence rather than threats to kill. That said, it is still a provision which *ought* to have been given consideration for use in dealing with some instances of online abuse, especially in light of the potential relaxing of the requirements as seen in *R (Hogle)*.

Other offences contained within the Public Order Act 1986 could also be potentially used to prosecute instances of social media threats. S4A(1)(a) of the POA[48] stipulates that a person will be guilty of an offence if, with an intent to cause a person harassment, alarm, or distress, he "uses threatening, abusive or insulting words or behaviour, or disorderly behaviour" which causes the other person harassment, alarm or distress. S4A(1)(b) makes it an offence to display writing or visible representations that are threatening, abusive, or insulting, and which causes as a result the person harassment, alarm, or distress. Again, on the surface, this could be of potential use in contemplating investigations and prosecutions of social media threats. That said – unlike s4 – there has been a significant level of judicial consideration of this provision and the required mental element necessary for a successful prosecution. It is a requirement that intention is present for an offence under s4A – namely that the words or behaviour should be threatening or abusive, or the defendant had an awareness that they may be threatening or abusive.[49]

It is also very much apparent that there is a distinction between a finding of offensive language and a finding of alarm and distress caused by that same offensive language. More so, it is significant that there has been judicial recognition that not everything which is offensive is distressing.[50] In *Smith*, the Court also indicated that it is open to the trial court to find that those who heard the words were caused or were likely to have been caused alarm or distress.[51] However, should a witness give evidence about the language used by a defendant but does not indicate whether they were caused harassment, alarm, or distress, there is no basis for a court to conclude that such harm has actually been caused. Irrespective of this, precedent indicates that the requirements of s4A will not be satisfied unless someone has heard the threatening or abusive language.[52] Again – much like s16 of the OAPA – the context in which the language or behaviour was used is an impor-

48 Enacted in February 1995 by the Criminal Justice and Public Order Act 1994, s 154.
49 POA 1986, s 6(4).
50 *DPP v Smith* [2017] EWHC 3193 (Admin). Hereafter, *Smith*.
51 ibid.
52 *Harvey v DPP* [2011] EWHC 3992 (Admin), [2012] Crim LR 553.

tant factor,[53] so much so that if the person to whom the behaviour or language is directed is frequently exposed to such language, then the impact of it may be lower.[54] Moreover, wherever there is swearing or similar language, that can be capable of causing harassment, alarm, or distress, but the question of whether it does so is likely to be a question of fact in any given case.[55] It is again – similar to s4 POA – unlikely that there will be a successful prosecution under s4A POA given the seemingly consistent requirement for the words to be heard.[56]

That said, it is not an inconceivable stretch to view written social media messages and threats as akin to words spoken – or shouted – and for potential prosecutions to therefore consider whether the necessary intent is present. This is a position which has gained some traction in more recent judicial thought. In *Taylor v DPP*,[57] the Court indicated that a person will be guilty of using threatening, abusive, or insulting words or behaviour within the hearing or sight of a person likely to be caused harassment, alarm, or distress thereby even if it could not be shown that someone did in fact hear the offending words.[58] It is, however, perfectly possible that even where there is a delay in the threats reaching the person against whom they were made, they can still cause harassment, distress, or alarm.[59] In *S v DPP,* the question arose as to whether harassment, alarm, or distress could be caused by a five month delay arising between the offending material being placed on the Internet and the complainant being shown hard copies by the police. The Court, in making its determination indicated that the defendant took the chance that the intended alarm or distress would be caused to the complainant and that it was therefore not material as to what had triggered the harassment, alarm, or distress. This is a clear indicator that one essential element is the harm caused, rather than the medium in which it is caused, with the second being intention. Newman, in particular, is of the opinion that: "[t]he intention of the appellant would be inferred due to the evidence of the taking of the photograph, the

53 *DPP v Orum* [1989] 1 WLR 88. Hereafter, *Orum*.

54 This is very much the position in respect of situations involving police officers who, according to the Court in *Orum*, were exposed to expletive and potentially threatening language frequently, and therefore, this was to be a factor given consideration in s 4A offences.

55 *Orum* (n 53); *Southard v DPP* [2006] EWHC 3449 (Admin).

56 The definition of "in sight or hearing of complainant" was established in *Chappell v DPP* (1989) Cr 82.

57 *Taylor v DPP* [2006] EWHC 1202 (Admin). Hereafter, *Taylor*.

58 There is no requirement for intention to satisfy an offence under POA 1986, s 5.

59 *S v DPP* [2008] EWHC 438 (Admin).

surrounding text, and the placing of it on a freely accessible website."[60] In such instances, it should be straightforward to identify the intention, thereby satisfying the requirements of a s4A offence. Consequently, this point is entirely relevant to social media threats – just because someone is a social media user does not mean that they necessarily will receive or view the threatening messages as soon as they are sent. It is irrespective whether there is a 'delay' in such circumstances, as the harm will still be caused when the person views the threatening message. There is some likelihood, however, that this suggestion would not be met with judicial support, particularly given that envelopes containing threats and abusive messages cannot be regarded as "displays" within the context of the POA offences because the messages are not displayed outside the envelope and are therefore effectively concealed messages.[61] As such, this suggests that there is some scope for non-oral threats to be considered here, especially given the "chameleon-like ability"[62] of the POA to adapt to behaviour which was not originally contemplated by the legislation.

Additionally, under s5 POA, there is a lesser offence which is prosecutable that also could be deployed in tackling social media threats. Under s5 – which is similar to, albeit distinct from, s4 and s4A POA – there is greater scope for behaviour to be assessed for its threatening or disorderly nature. For a s5(1)(a) offence to occur, there must be threatening words or behaviour, or disorderly behaviour used by a person to cause or be likely to cause harassment to another person. A s5(1)(b)[63] offence will be committed where a person displays threatening visible representations likely to cause harassment, alarm, or distress. Both of these offences differ from s4 and s4A offences in that there is no requirement of intention to satisfy for s5 offences.[64] Additionally, behaviour which contributes to "a breakdown of peaceful and law-abiding behaviour as evidenced by the reactions of the public"[65] is likely to be sufficient to satisfy the requirements of a s5 offence. Specifically, here it is unnecessary to determine whether the defendant actually was threatening, abusive, or insulting because the

60 Chris Newman, 'Offensive Picture on the Internet Later Shown to Complainant by a Third Party Causing Distress' (2008) 72 JCL 481.

61 *Chappell* (n 56).

62 Newman, 'Offensive Picture on the Internet Later Shown to Complainant by a Third Party Causing Distress' (n 60).

63 The original drafting of this provision included 'abusive' displays but the wording – namely 'abusive' – was substituted by the Crime and Courts Act 2013, s 57(2), enacted in February 2014.

64 *Smith* (n 50).

65 *Gough v DPP* [2013] EWHC 3267 (Admin), where the defendant had been charged under s 5 for walking naked through a town. Hereafter, *Gough*.

actions of the defendant can lead to conclusions of disorderly behaviour and thereby satisfy s5(1)(a). It is equally clear that the courts will assess each case on its own merits as to whether the behaviour complained of is sufficient to satisfy s5.[66] The conviction in *Gough* is surprising[67] because, on the surface of it, walking through towns naked is rather trivial behaviour and yet can give rise to alarm and distress which is sufficient to pursue a prosecution. It is therefore a sorry state of affairs that this behaviour can give rise to clear criminal liability – and perhaps more significantly here – give rise to the kind of harassment and distress that the state believes worthy of punishing. This is an incomprehensible dichotomy when compared to the harm inflicted by social media threats and abuse, which it seems, is much more difficult for the criminal law to recognise.

Interestingly, the problems caused by the triviality of the behaviour in *Gough* have potentially significant ramifications here. The judge in *Gough* is of the opinion that words such as 'insulting' must be given full consideration:

> 'insulting' and by extrapolation, 'threatening', 'abusive' and 'disorderly' are not to be narrowly construed (. . .) that 'insulting' meant disrespectful or scornful abuse, 'threatening' was behaviour that was hostile, had a deliberately frightening quality or manner or which caused someone to feel vulnerable or at risk. 'Abusive' meant extremely offensive and insulting, and 'disorderly behaviour' was behaviour that involved or contributed to a breakdown of peaceful and law-abiding behaviour.[68]

This is a distinct discussion to that offered in *Chambers and Edwards v DPP*, [69] where the courts indicated that harassment, alarm, and distress were all alternative terms. Moreover, in order for disorderly behaviour to exist, there was no requirement of any violence – either intended or actual; and conduct which is not necessarily threatening could be included. However, if someone were to repeatedly shout abuse or obscenities, that could be disorderly conduct for the purposes of s5.[70] Evidently, given the definitions considered in *Gough*, the previous position sees a development

66 ibid.

67 Nick Taylor, 'Gough (Stephen Peter) v Director of Public Prosecutions: Public Order – Appellant Walking Nude through a Town Centre. Divisional Court; PQBD Sir Brian Leveson and Openshaw J: October 31; [2013] EWHC 3267 (Admin)' (2014) 5 Crim LR 371, 373.

68 *Gough* (n 65) [10] (Sir Brian Leveson P).

69 *Chambers and Edwards v DPP* [1995] Crim LR 896.

70 ibid; Pat Strickland and Diana Douse, '"Insulting Words or Behaviour": Section 5 of the Public Order Act 1986' (*House of Commons Library*, Commons Briefing Paper

to a situation where the words connote different behaviours. Despite these definitions, swearing in public – particularly using 'fuck' or 'fucking' – includes the use of potentially abusive words. This remains the situation in the absence of a specific offence of swearing in public.[71] If swearing alone is sufficient to indicate disorderly behaviour then, again, there is reason to consider using s5 to prosecute social media threats.

Attached to this – and to s5 POA in particular following *Gough* – are understandable concerns surrounding the interference with human rights, including Article 10 rights. Whilst these concerns can rightly be raised here, *Gough* focuses on an expression not of speech or opinion, but of personal autonomy. Accordingly, this expression is still subjected to protection but is also subjected to more legitimate restrictions than other more valuable forms of expression.[72] In the words of Baroness Hale:

> There are undoubtedly different kinds of speech (. . .) some of which are more deserving of protection in a democratic society than others. Top of the list is political speech. The free exchange of information and ideas on matters relevant to the organisation of the economic, social and political life of the country is crucial to any democracy.[73]

Free expression concerns aside, there is considerable scope under the POA to lodge prosecutions for social media threats, subject to the hurdles in s4, s4A and s5 that there needs to be someone within hearing or sight of the person making the threats or showing threatening behaviour. This remains the position despite some subtle judicial consideration suggesting that there is some flexibility creeping in to the legislative scope of the offences. Even where there is some emerging flexibility, the reality is that the requirements of physical presence and immediacy are incredibly limiting for threats sent via social media. These requirements – despite judicial nudges towards expansions of the behaviours covered by the s4, s4A, and s5 offences – render the POA provisions practically useless for social media threats. Simple rewording of the offences could readily make them available for use in tackling pernicious, offensive, and threatening behaviour on social media platforms.[74]

SN05760, 15 January 2013) < https://researchbriefings.parliament.uk/ResearchBriefing/Summary/SN05760#fullreport> accessed 10 September 2018, 4.

71 *Harvey* (n 52). The authors are not advocating for a specific offence of swearing in public.

72 Taylor, 'Gough (Stephen Peter) v Director of Public Prosecutions' (n 67) 373.

73 *Campbell v Mirror Group Newspapers* [2004] UKHL 22, 148 (Lady Hale).

74 Other provisions within the existing legislation also purport to deal with threats, including the Malicious Communications Act 1988, s 1. See below at *3.7. Communications networks* for discussion.

Part II

Stalking and harassment

For situations involving social media abuse, but where the reprehensible behaviour falls short of the making of threats to kill, it is possible to perceive that the activity may amount to stalking. The current offences of stalking are found in the Protection from Harassment Act 1997.[75] This piece of legislation was originally intended to take the form of a Stalking Bill[76] which, in the words of the CPS, "was always intended to tackle all forms of harassment."[77] Unfortunately, the Bill was regarded as ambiguous when it was considered at its Second Reading and therefore there has been a need to refer to the comments made in the House of Lords to offer some insight into the composition of the offences and the aim of the Act itself.[78] Given the problematic origins of the Act, it has undergone a number of significant reforms – both to address weaknesses within it, but also to reflect changing understandings of behaviour which is reprehensible enough that society requires criminal sanctions to be levied in response.[79] The original drafting of the Act was amended in 2005[80] so as to rectify – or at least aim to rectify – the perception held by victims of incidents of stalking that their claims were not being appropriately considered by the criminal law. The changes were further enhanced by the Protection of Freedoms Act 2012[81] which introduced two new offences to the PHA which were specifically intended to offer greater protection to stalking victims.

75 Hereafter PHA 1997.

76 See 'Stalking Legislation' at CPS, 'Stalking and Harassment' (*Crown Prosecution Service*, last updated 23 May 2018) <www.cps.gov.uk/legal-guidance/stalking-and-harassment> accessed 10 September 2018.

77 ibid. Note that discussions of the more generalised criminal behaviour of harassment – in particular discussions of ss 2 and 4 of the PHA 1997 – will therefore be limited in this section. These are discussed in detail below at 3.6 Harassment.

78 On the basis of a *Pepper v Hart* note.

79 See, for example, Lord Chancellor, Lord Mackay of Clashfern in the House of Lords in 1997: HL Deb 24 January 1997, vol 577, col 918. See also below at 3.6. Harassment.

80 The PHA 1997 was amended by the Serious Organised Crime and Police Act 2005, s 125(3) (hereafter, SOCPA 2005) on 1 July 2005.

81 Hereafter, PFA 2012.

3.5 Stalking

S111 PFA introduced into the PHA offences which make stalking a specific behaviour, rather than having to rely on harassment in a more general context for a successful claim to be made. The offences contained within the PHA in s2A and s4A are the new offences which have been introduced to address shortcomings in this area. Whilst it is a positive development to see such reforms introduced, the use of the provisions to take prosecution action is still something that requires improvement. In 2015, for instance, the Crime Survey for England and Wales identified that 734 000 women reported stalking.[82] Beyond this, the prosecution rates under the PHA offences are somewhat limited. Between 2012 and 2015, only 1975 people were prosecuted under s2A PHA or s4A PHA. More concerningly, only 1273 of these 1975 were convicted.[83] In s2A and s4A, there are now dedicated offences for the activity of stalking – and these mirror the pre-existing offences in s2 and 4 of harassment.

The new s4A PHA also introduces an additional element allowing cases to be prosecuted under s4A(1)(b)(ii) even where the behaviour of the defendant falls short of the required threshold to prove that there has been a fear of violence inflicted upon the victim. The critical distinction here between the new s4A(1)(b)(ii) offence and the s4 harassment offence is that the cumulative effect can be considered without the need for specific incidents which are particularly serious. This is a significant change to the legislative framework and one which can be hugely beneficial to victims of stalking providing the prosecution services are willing – and able – to pursue prosecutions. Prior to the amendments, where there was an inability to demonstrate that the defendant had caused fear of violence, there could only be a summary charge pursued under the less serious s2 offence – again, failing the victims in instances of stalking. The introduction of new offences also specifically identifies stalking as a standalone behaviour rather than including it within the more generic behaviour of 'harassment'. This distinction is a particularly useful one in the context of social media incidents, particularly because if there is now a standalone behaviour of stalking this *should* allow for generic behaviour to be the subject of criminal proceedings too. As such, arguably these law reforms have made the position slightly easier when it comes to online text-based abuses. That said, the PHA

82 Suzy Lamplugh Trust, 'Managing Stalking Offenders' (*Suzy Lamplugh Trust*) <www.suzylamplugh.org/managing-stalking-offenders> accessed 10 September 2018.

83 ibid.

provisions are far from straightforward and drawing a distinction between harassment and stalking is often blurry and messy.

Under s2A, a person will be found guilty of stalking if the conduct – as in s2 – breaches s1(1) and that course of conduct results in stalking. Unlike s2, with its absence of harassment definition, the s2A offence defines what is likely to be deemed as behaviour equating to stalking. Specifically, a person will be guilty of stalking if the behaviour amounts to harassment,[84] and it is associated with stalking,[85] and the person conducting the behaviour knows or is aware that the behaviour is harassing.[86] Whilst there has been little judicial consideration given specifically to the s2A offence, the references within s2A make explicit links to the considerations of harassment envisaged for satisfying the requirements of s2 and 4. In addition, s2A(3) offers some examples of the kinds of behaviour which will (if harassing) amount to a conviction under s2A for stalking.

Notably, in the context of social media abuse and online harassment, this includes: "contacting, or attempting to contact a person by any means."[87] This alone will fall short of the activity required to sustain a conviction for stalking. The behaviour complained of must also satisfy the requirements of harassment. In other words, trying simply to contact someone – for example, through Twitter – is not enough. To satisfy s2A, the contact must be: harassing;[88] targeted at an individual; calculated to cause alarm, or distress to the individual; and oppressive, and unreasonable.[89] The conduct must also have occurred on at least two occasions. If these elements are all satisfied, then a s2A offence could be proved. Given the close correlation, but increased seriousness of a s2A offence, it is difficult to see why prosecutions for social media stalking do not also occur. Additionally, given the severity of the harm caused to victims of social media abuse, the more serious offences should be pursued. The severity – and consequences – of behaviour amounting to stalking is evident in the increased sentencing which follows such a s2A conviction – up to 51 weeks in prison.[90] Finally, whilst the introduction of specific offences is intended to address behaviours of greater seriousness, they potentially could be detrimental to the generality of the s2

84 PHA 1997, s 2A(2)(a).

85 ibid, s 2A(2)(b).

86 ibid, s 2A(2)(c).

87 ibid, s 2A(3)(b).

88 Explanatory Notes to the Protection for Freedoms Act 2012, para 446. The indicative list of behaviours was taken from the Criminal Justice and Licensing Act (Scotland) 2010 (asp 13), s 39.

89 *Thomas v News Group Newspapers Ltd* [2001] EWCA Civ 1235 (per Lord Phillips MR).

90 PHA 1997, s 2A(4).

offence. Fortunately, this problem is largely circumvented by the fall-back position which s2 offers in the event that a prosecution under s2A fails to evidence the stalking behaviour but still proves the harassment. This approach – in the absence of social media specific provisions – potentially offers the greatest balance between generality and severity and allows – if utilised – more potential routes to redress for victims.

In any event, the reforms made to this area of law – inspired by the more robust stance adopted in Scots Law[91] – are a positive and welcome development,[92] even if the drafting of the provisions could be further improved.[93] Of course, the legislative and justice system elements of these offences are only two aspects – and reactive ones at that – other multifaceted considerations ought to be made so that users of social media are aware that the digital sphere too attracts sanctions.[94]

The stalking offence in s4A mirrors the more serious of the harassment offences in s4. The s4A offence shares the requirement of "involving fear of violence or serious alarm or distress" with s4. Consequently, where there is a course of conduct amounting to stalking[95] and that causes someone else to fear that violence will be used against him on at least two occasions,[96] or the conduct causes serious alarm or distress to the extent that it has a "substantial adverse effect on B's usual day-to-day activities"[97] that person will be guilty of an offence. This phrase is not defined within the PHA and is therefore left to judicial interpretation. Some guidance on this point is derivable from the Home Office Guidelines which indicate that there is likely to be a substantial adverse effect where – for example – a victim changes their daily patterns, changes social engagements, and puts in place additional security measures at home, or moves.[98] Several factors from this non-exhaustive but indicative list were steps taken by Criado-Perez and Creasy in light of the harassment they suffered. This is, perhaps, further evidence that there ought to have been a prosecution under a more substantive criminal provision such as this one.

91 The indicative list of behaviours was taken from the Criminal Justice and Licensing Act (Scotland) 2010 (asp 13), s 39.

92 Neil MacEwan, 'The New Stalking Offences in English law: Will They Provide Effective Protection from Cyberstalking?' [2012] 10 Crim LR 767, 780.

93 ibid.

94 Jennifer Agate and Jocelyn Ledward, 'Social Media: How the Net is Closing in on Cyber Bullies' (2013) 24 EntLR 263, 267.

95 PHA 1997, s 4A(1)(a).

96 ibid, s 4A(1)(b)(i).

97 ibid, s 4A(1)(b)(ii).

98 Home Office, 'Circular: A Change to the Protection from Harassment Act 1997' (HM Government, Home Office Circular 018/2012, 16 October 2012) <www.gov.uk/government/publications/a-change-to-the-protection-from-harassment-act-1997-introduction-of-two-new-specific-offences-of-stalking> accessed 10 September 2018.

Returning to the substantive offences in the PHA, in a manner similar to the correlations between s2 and s2A, the s4A offence shares key elements with s4, including the objective test of the reasonable person to adduce whether the conduct is of a sufficient level to satisfy the requirements of the offence. The s4A offence also relies on s4 as a fallback position whereby a conviction for harassment under s4 can be found by the jury if there is a failure to evidence the fear of violence for a s4A conviction. Should a s4A prosecution be successful, a sentence of up to five years[99] or up to 12-months[100] can be imposed, or for instances where there are multiple victims, consecutive sentences can be imposed.[101]

There is still a requirement – as part of the s4A offence – to determine the material consequences of the stalking behaviours in a particular case. Given the references made to harassment-style activity in s7, which includes "alarming a person, or causing the person distress"[102] these elements also retain a role in establishing the course of conduct against which there is a prohibition. The s4A offences also require – like s4 – considerations of the immediacy of the fear of violence. The *Qosja*[103] court has made it clear that in relation to s4A, there is no requirement for the fear to be of violence on a particular date or time in the future. By extension, there is no requirement for the fear of violence to be at a specific place, in a particular form, nor for specific threats to be made.[104] The critical criterion is that the victim fears that there will[105] be at least two occasions where violence is directed at them. This is a point which is particularly important for social media abuse which amounts to stalking, especially where that abuse causing fear of violence is sent electronically from unknown communicators in unknown locations.

More significantly, the 2017 amendments to s4A increase the maximum possible custodial sentence to one of five years[106] – a significant indicator that the justice system finally recognises the impact that stalking offences can have. This is equally applicable to stalking offences committed through social media. Consequently, given that these offences were

99 PHA 1997 s 4A(5)(a), for conviction on indictment. This was amended by the Policing and Crime Act 2017, s 175(1)(b).

100 PHA 1997, s 4A(5)(b) for a summary conviction.

101 *R v Danevska* [2017] EWCA Crim 1084.

102 PHA 1997, s 7(2); *R v Tan* [2017] EWCA Crim 493 (per Sir Brian Leveson P).

103 *R v Qosja* [2016] EWCA Crim 1543.

104 *R v Henley* [2000] Crim LR 582 CA (Crim Div); *R (A Child) v DPP* [2001] EWHC 17 (Admin).

105 The statutory requirement for the fear of violence is *will* rather than *may* (emphasis added). Zach Leggatt, 'Now or Never? How Imminent Must a Fear of Violence Be for the Purposes of s 4A of the Protection from Harassment Act 1997? R v Qosja (Robert)' (2017) 81 JCL 17, 19.

106 Amended by Policing and Crime Act 2017, s 175(1)(b).

enacted at the time Criado-Perez and Creasy were subjected to harassment and stalking, it is difficult to comprehend why prosecutions were not pursued under such provisions. Whilst the authors accept that the alterations to the sentencing period were not enacted at the time of sentencing, custodial sentences of 8 and 12 weeks respectively for Nimmo and Sorley seem rather light given the impact their harassment had on their victims.

The conduct amounting to harassment which is envisaged by provisions dealing with 'threats' within the Offences Against the Person Act 1861 and the Public Order Act 1986 is distinct from that considered to fall within the Protection from Harassment Act 1997, specifically s2 and s4.[107] The use of the same term to connote different conduct is one of the problems in regulating this broad area and is further confused within the context of the POA 1986 by the judgment in *Chambers and Edwards v DPP* [1995] which indicates that the terms 'harassment', 'abuse', and 'distress' are alternatives.[108] These terms appear in numerous statutes and judgments, and are all seemingly used interchangeably with little focus being given to the precise parameters and meanings of the behaviour in question. This compounds the existing regulatory difficulties in the area of social media abuse and threats, specifically because the behaviours in question have minor distinctions between them, yet these are not reflected in the legal provisions nor in judicial interpretations. Interchangeability can in some instances lead to flexibility within the law – yet in the context of social media, it leads to a confused and messy legal situation that lacks clarity and further fails sufferers.

3.6 Harassment

Where social media behaviour does not involve activities of stalking, nor making threats, it may – and could – still fall within the remit of the criminal law, in particular, through provisions dealing with conduct amounting to harassment.[109] The Protection from Harassment Act 1997 was introduced to deal with problematic conduct which is "sufficiently reprehensible for society to express its disapproval."[110] In the words of the then Lord Chancellor, "Criminal sanctions are necessary so that victims can call upon the police to investigate instances of harassment, particularly where the identity of the person causing the harassment is

107 See above at 3.5. Stalking.
108 See above at 3.4. Threats and threats to kill.
109 The provisions within the Public Order Act 1986 addressing behaviours which may amount to harassment are discussed above at 3.4. Threats and threats to kill.
110 HL Deb 24 January 1997, vol 577, col 918 (Lord Chancellor, Lord Mackay of Clashfern).

not known to the victim."[111] The view taken in 1997 shows recognition of the need to address behaviour which causes distress or alarm to the victim, most especially when the person causing that distress is unknown – quite frequently the exact situation which (now) occurs in the context of social media abuse. Given that the type of conduct in the contemplation of the Government at the time the PHA was drafted included conduct which causes distress and disturbance, it is not a stretch to see why social media messages which lead to distress or alarm should now also fall within the remit of this legislation. Again though – much like the situation in respect of the OAPA – no prosecution was advanced under the PHA in the landmark case of *R v Nimmo & Sorley*. The original legislation was intended to be focussed on stalking but given the problems with that Act – specifically the lack of a specific offence of stalking – much needed amendments were enacted by the PFA 2012. A further prohibition was introduced in 2005[112] to allow for offences amounting to pursuing conduct against two or more people,[113] or that which is intended to persuade someone to do that which he is not obliged to do,[114] or to persuade someone not to do something he is entitled or required to do.[115] The requirements for prohibiting conduct being pursued against more than one individual are the same as for pursuing an individual.[116]

Under the PHA, s1 stipulates a prohibition – not a criminal offence – against pursuing a course of conduct which amounts to harassment,[117] or which a person ought to know amounts to harassment.[118] Offences established in s1 are enforced by s2 and it is the enforcement of that section which gives rise to criminal sanctions – an unusual feature of this legislation. The revised legislative framework now draws a distinction between conduct which is regarded as sufficiently serious to amount to harassment and that which, whilst still significant, fails to be as serious and is therefore classified as stalking.[119] The prohibition

111 ibid.

112 PHA 1997, s 1(1A) was introduced by the SOCPA 2005, s 125(2)(a), enacted 1 July 2005. Subsequent amendments were made to PHA 1997 s 1 by the PFA 2012, enacted 25 November 2012.

113 PHA 1997, s 1(A)(a)

114 ibid, s 1(1A)(c)(ii).

115 ibid, s 1(1A)(c)(i).

116 The discussion of the requirements of the prohibition in s 1, and the enforcement in s 2 will therefore not distinguish between conduct pursued against an individual and conduct pursued against individuals.

117 PHA 1997, ss 1(a) and 2.

118 ibid, ss 1(b) and 2.

119 This statement does not intentionally belittle either form of behaviour, or the harms flowing from such conduct. The point here is that there is a legal distinction

contained within s1 – and enforced by s2 – is one of pursuing a 'course of conduct' which 'amounts to' harassment[120] or which the defendant knows amounts to harassment.[121] Under s2, a conviction will result in a custodial sentence of no more than six months.

For a s2 conviction, it is a requirement to demonstrate that harassment has taken place. There is – unhelpfully – no definition of what is meant by 'harassment' within the PHA. That said, the indicative definition which was introduced in 2005 (when the PHA was amended) suggests that the harassment required must give rise to "a course of conduct which harasses or alarms another or which causes that person distress."[122] In addition, to achieve a conviction, the conduct must occur at least two times. The courts have interpreted these requirements strictly[123] so as to limit the breadth of potential convictions. That said, given the requirements of the conduct, it is difficult to perceive reasons why there have not been any high-profile convictions under s2 PHA for social media abuse. This is especially so given that the sending of threatening and vitriolic messages across several hours and days which are sufficiently distressing and alarming as to cause victims – such as Criado-Perez and Creasy – to leave their homes would seem to more than satisfy the requirements of the offence.

Despite this, judicial considerations of the nuances of s2 offer some insights as to why there are limited prosecutions. Whilst it is not expressly stated in s2, it is abundantly clear that there is a requirement of targeting which ought to be satisfied.[124] The element of targeting does not require the targeting of a specific individual – a point clarified in *Levi v Bates.*[125] In that case, Willcox indicated: "that Parliament cannot have intended to exclude by implication those people who would be foreseeably alarmed and distressed by a course of conduct of the targeted type contemplated by the word harassment."[126] By reaching such a conclusion – and in *Levi*, Briggs LJ disagreed with the earlier judgment of Simon J in *Dowson*[127] who suggested that it had to be established that the

between the consequences of each type of behaviour something that has only recently been recognised in the statutory provisions.

120 PHA 1997, s 1(a).

121 ibid, s 1(b).

122 Explanatory Notes to the Serious Organised Crime and Police Act 2005, para 303.

123 ibid.

124 *Thomas* (n 89).

125 [2015] EWCA Civ 206. Hereafter, *Levi*.

126 Rebecca Willcox, '*Levi v Bates* – Harassment and the Concept of Targeted Behaviour' (2015) 26 EntLR 209.

127 *Dowson v Chief Constable of Northumbria Police* [2010] EWHC 2612 (QB). Hereafter, *Dowson*.

claimant was the intended target of the conduct – Briggs LJ has limited the potential range of claimants under s2 to those who are: (1) intended victims of the harassment; and (2) not the intended victims but those "foreseeably and directly harmed by the course of targeted conduct."[128] Consequently, if the defendant knows or ought to know that his conduct amounts to harassment he will be liable to the person harassed irrespective of whether or not the conduct is targeted at another. Whilst this has fewer implications in offline instances of distressing and abusive behaviour, in a social media context, the target element is one which ought to operate in closer alignment to the – now – unfavoured approach of Simon LJ in *Dowson*. This is most especially because social media abuse is directed at specific individuals – and is *intended*[129] to be.

There is however, more to the conduct requirement than that it causes harm – directly or indirectly. In order to achieve a criminal conviction, there has to be conduct which is more than "merely unattractive or unreasonable" and it must cross the boundary into behaviour which is "oppressive and unacceptable."[130] More simply, there is a certain level of irritation that has to be tolerated before the law – especially the criminal law – will intervene,[131] a point reiterated by Toulson LJ, who stated that: "[i]t does not follow that because references to harassing a person include alarming a person or causing a person distress . . . any course of conduct which causes alarm or distress therefore amounts to harassment."[132] The meaning of harass was also considered at length in 2010 by the Court of Appeal, which – similarly to the judgment of Toulson LJ – applied a practical approach to the issue by following a dictionary definition in stating that: "[t]o harass . . . is to 'torment by subjecting to constant interference or intimidation.'"[133]

In reality therefore, there are a number of approaches – albeit similar ones – that offer insights as to the precise conduct that has to occur for harassment under s2 to be found. Ultimately, that conduct has to be serious. Beyond that, to satisfy the full requirements of the offence, the behaviour complained of must occur on at least two occasions otherwise there is no establishment of the necessary course of conduct. This has been taken to mean that to satisfy the requirement, the behaviour must be

128 *Levi* (n 125) [34] (Briggs LJ).

129 Emphasis added.

130 *Majrowski v Guy's and St Thomas' NHS Trust* [2005] EWCA Civ 251 [82] (May LJ); *Calland v FCA* [2015] EWCA Civ 192 [5] (Lewison J).

131 *Ferguson v British Gas Trading Ltd* [2009] EWCA Civ 46 [17] (Jacob LJ). Hereafter, *Ferguson*.

132 *R v Smith (Mark)* [2012] EWCA Crim 2566 [24].

133 *R v Curtis* [2010] EWCA Crim 123 [29] (Pill LJ).

related on the two – or more – occasions in both type and context.[134] The judicial assessment of what is required to satisfy a course of conduct has been considered very broadly.[135] This is in stark contrast to what has been considered as harassment. Despite the broad considerations given to what is meant by course of conduct, it is notable that the definition has been left this way by design. In *Majrowski*, for example, Baroness Hale noted that the definition: "had been deliberately left wide open and it had been left to the wisdom of the courts to distinguish between the ordinary banter and badinage of life and genuinely offensive and unacceptable behaviour."[136]

Similarly, the context in which the alleged harassing incidents have occurred is also a significant consideration for the courts.[137] Furthermore, it is irrelevant that there have been only two incidents of a particular course of conduct. Where this is the situation, it is these incidents – assuming that they are connected in type and context – which must be considered to establish whether they are capable of constituting a course of conduct.[138] Of course, should there be two incidents that appear connected in type and context, where they have happened with a gap in time, that may be sufficient to indicate that they do not comprise a course of conduct.[139] This is the situation despite the absence of any time correlation for the conduct appearing in the legislation as part of the requirements to satisfy a s2 offence. That said, the courts must bear in mind that they are deciding on whether or not the behaviour in question falls into the category of harassment.[140] It is important to remember that, "[t]he mischief, which the Act is intended to meet, is that persons should not be put in a state of alarm or distress by repetitious behaviour."[141] If this summary is accurate, then at its simplest, the s2 provision should be capable of being used to pursue prosecutions for abuse levied at users of social media platforms, especially if the aim of the provision is to prevent an individual suffering alarm or distress through repetitive behaviour which is deemed reprehensible enough to attract attention from the criminal justice system.

The s2 offence is not the only offence which appears in the PHA with harassment and a 'course of conduct' at its core. The criminal offence

134 *R v Patel* [2005] 1 Cr App R 27; *James v DPP* [2009] EWHC 2925 (Admin) [11] (Elias LJ).

135 David Ormerod, 'Case Comment: *James v DPP:* Harassment – Appellant Phoning Social Services – Victim Not Available to Take Appellant's Calls – Victim Later Returning Phone Calls' (2010) 7 Crim LR 580, 581.

136 *Majrowski* (n 130) [66] (Lady Hale).

137 *Conn v Sunderland City Council* [2007] EWCA Civ 1492 (per Gage LJ).

138 *Lau v DPP* [2000] 1 FLR 799 (per Schiemann LJ).

139 *Pratt v DPP* [2001] EWHC Admin 483.

140 *C v CPS* [2008] EWHC 148 (Admin).

141 *Pratt* (n 139) [10] (Latham LJ).

introduced in s4 is one which operates at a "higher level"[142] than the offence in s2. For a successful prosecution under s4, the course of conduct in question does not refer to behaviour which is "grossly offensive and unacceptable,"[143] rather it requires a course of conduct that "causes another to fear, on at least two occasions, that violence will be used against him."[144] Therefore, the conduct necessary here is that which puts people in fear of violence being used against them.[145] The requirement will be satisfied – on the basis of an objective test – if a reasonable person who has the same knowledge and information as the victim would believe the conduct to cause fear.[146] Consequently, the distinction between the s2 offence and the s4 offence rests on the violence aspect required in the latter. This too is a provision of potential use in instances concerning social media abuse, particularly where the messages sent via social media are particularly aggressive, menacing, or even threatening. Several of the messages communicated to Criado-Perez and Creasy suggest violence without containing threats that are sufficient to satisfy the provisions within the OAPA, or the POA.

Where a successful conviction is lodged for a s4 PHA offence, there is a maximum sentence (if convicted on indictment) of 10 years[147] or six months (if a summary conviction).[148] Interestingly, in situations where the required course of conduct demonstrating fear of violence cannot be established – and no s4 conviction is forthcoming – a jury may still find a defendant guilty of a s2 offence of harassment. The s4 provision therefore utilises the lesser offence as a fall-back position – which makes it even more inexplicable that those provisions have yet to be deployed to tackle social media abuse.

The original interpretation of s4 referred to the element of harassment[149] – even though the current legislative wording does not.[150] As such, s4 remains an offence of harassment[151] but the harassment

142 HL Deb 24 January 1997, vol 577, col 920 (Lord Chancellor, Lord Mackay of Clashfern).
143 *Majrowski* (n 130) [66] (Lady Hale).
144 PHA 1997, s 4(1).
145 ibid.
146 ibid, s 4(2).
147 ibid, s 4(4)(a).
148 ibid, s 4(4)(b).
149 "Where the level of harassment is such that a person is caused to fear violence, the Government believe that the higher penalties provided by this clause . . . are appropriate. . . . It cannot be reasonable to place someone in fear of violence." HL Deb 24 January 1997, vol 577, col 920 (Lord Chancellor, Lord Mackay of Clashfern).
150 *R v Widdows* [2011] EWCA Crim 1500 [30] (Pill LJ).
151 *Thomas* (n 89).

required – despite its controversy[152] – is that of causing fear of violence. Indeed, the court in *Haque* initially intended to take a more relaxed approach to the requirements of the s4 offence given the broad definitions used within s1. Unfortunately, the intent of the court in *Haque* to treat s4 as "a freestanding offence and [one that] does not require proof of harassment"[153] was rendered impossible. Notably, Lord Phillips MR indicated that there was no such interpretation available to s4 and that to succeed in a conviction, the prosecution requires proof: (1) of harassment; (2) that the conduct in question was targeted at an individual (not necessarily the claimant); (3) that the conduct was calculated to alarm or cause distress to the targeted individual; and (4) that the conduct was oppressive and unreasonable.[154] These requirements must – in the opinion of Lord Phillips MR – be established in addition to the statutory requirements of s4; namely that the conduct leads to a fear of violence, established through the objective test.

The difficulties of establishing what is meant by a course of conduct under s2 are also abundant for considerations of s4, precisely because there is a requirement for a course of conduct to be established irrespective of the section. In essence, the heart of the PHA rests on first establishing harassment and only then, second, the nature of that harassment because, "both [sections] are concerned with a course of conduct amounting to harassment."[155] The complexity of the relationship between the two sections and establishing harassment is neatly summarised by Pill LJ who states that: "[t]he two limbs are inter-related in that an analysis of the course of conduct, including the frequency of the acts, may well throw light on whether it amounts to harassment."[156]

S4 – much like its s2 counterpart – can be equally useful in situations where social media abuse is under scrutiny. Whilst the abuse may not reach the standards required for a s4 conviction, given the ready availability of s2 as a fall-back lesser offence, serious questions must be asked of the prosecution service, who, it would seem, have been unwilling or unable to use all of the relevant provisions in the statute book to tackle the harms caused by social media abuse – especially where that abuse amounts to a course of conduct sufficient to demonstrate harassment.

152 *R v Haque* [2011] EWCA Crim 1871 (hereafter, *Haque)*; *Widdows* (n 150).
153 *Haque*, ibid [69] (Hooper LJ).
154 *Thomas* (n 89).
155 *Curtis* (n 133) [20] (Pill LJ).
156 ibid [31] (Pill LJ).

Part III

Communications

In the absence of social media behaviour which is sufficiently serious and which could fall within the scope of the offences contained within the OAPA, POA, and PHA, there may be the potential to pursue a prosecution on the basis of a communications offence rather than another – more substantive – offence. This point is not sugar-coated by the CPS – who publicly acknowledge the fact in their prosecutorial guidelines[157] – and yet, the broader implications here suggest that consideration ought always to be given to the prosecution of a substantive offence – such as, for example, harassment[158] – before the communications provisions are relied upon, especially as these offences (whilst less substantive criminally), will be very difficult to satisfy in terms of the public interest. The wider inference from such an admission by the CPS is that social media behaviour is much less serious than so-called 'offline' behaviour and that is reflected in the approaches to prosecutions. Yet despite this, the most high-profile social media abuse cases have not been considered alongside the more substantive offences and instead, the communications provisions have been the only ones used – especially notable in *R v Nimmo & Sorley*[159] and *R v Viscount St Davids*.[160]

3.7 Communications networks

If the communications provisions are to be prominently relied upon to address issues of social media abuse – and substantive offences are to be overlooked, as has been the trend to date – then these provisions must be fit for purpose. There are several key provisions in the communications legislation that are relevant to discussions of social media abuse, depending upon the precise actions that are in question. Unlike with the substantive offences, there is little doubt that these provisions can be utilised against social media abuse. The difficulties here do not lie in establishing that social media abuse falls within their remit – quite the

157 CPS, 'Social Media – Guidelines on Prosecuting Cases Involving Communications Sent via Social Media' (*Crown Prosecution Service*, revised 21 August 2018) <www.cps.gov.uk/legal-guidance/social-media-guidelines-prosecuting-cases-involving-communications-sent-social-media> accessed 10 September 2018, para 10.

158 See above at 3.6. Harassment.

159 (n 16).

160 (n 17).

opposite – the difficulties here lie in establishing sufficiently lengthy sentences and in adequately dealing with the misuse of the communications networks. As such, the communications provisions have no real scope for considering the full harm caused by a person who seeks to send offensive or distressing communications. The emphasis in this area does not rest on the activity of the accused in terms of a course of conduct – rather it rests on the physical act of sending a communication. Both s1 of the Malicious Communications Act[161] and s127 of the Communications Act[162] are offences of sending.[163]

Under the MCA, the offences contained within it are those of sending any communications – including electronic communications – which convey indecent or grossly offensive messages,[164] or threats,[165] or electronic communications which are wholly or partly indecent or grossly offensive.[166] In addition, the communication must cause distress or anxiety to the person receiving it[167] – if no harm in this manner arises, then it will be difficult to persuade a jury that the requirements of a MCA offence have been satisfied. Original case law under the MCA did not place an emphasis on social media issues for the obvious reason that the legislation predates social media platforms. Nevertheless, courts have had to consider the meaning of "grossly offensive" within the s1 context and have made it clear that there is no special meaning given to the phrase.[168]

Moreover, whilst electronic communications now include those sent via social media platforms between users, there is a sharp distinction to be drawn between posts made on social media or interactive online platforms – which do not necessarily involve the 'sending' of a communication – and those which are sent directly to identified users. Above all, the 'sending' is the required act for s1 offences and that is defined as delivering or transmitting.[169] This must be accompanied

161 Malicious Communications Act 1988, as amended. Hereafter, MCA 1988.

162 Communications Act 2003. Hereafter, CA 2003.

163 CPS, 'Social Media – Guidelines on Prosecuting Cases Involving Communications Sent via Social Media' (*Crown Prosecution Service*, revised 21 August 2018) <www.cps.gov.uk/legal-guidance/social-media-guidelines-prosecuting-cases-involving-communications-sent-social-media> accessed 10 September 2018.

164 MCA 1988, s 1(a)(i).

165 ibid, s 1(a)(ii). For a fuller discussion of substantive criminal offences dealing with threats, see above at 3.4. Threats and threats to kill.

166 ibid, s 1(b).

167 ibid, s 1.

168 *Connolly v DPP* [2007] EWHC 237 (Admin).

169 MCA 1988, s 3.

by the required mental element – which for s1 offences here is that the sender of the message had as their purpose the causing of distress or anxiety to the intended recipient.[170] Provided that the elements of this offence have been satisfied, if someone posts an undirected tweet on their own Twitter feed, this may not satisfy the offence. The key issue in such situations rests on the likelihood of the intended recipient receiving the communication. Consequently, the s1 threshold is very high and only if fully satisfied will a defendant receive a custodial sentence of up to two years.[171] Despite the clear understanding of the very high threshold – a point again accepted by the CPS[172] – the resultant maximum sentence is only a fraction of that available in instances where threats – or harassment – perpetrated through electronic means is treated as a substantive criminal offence.[173]

The need under s1 for a communication to be grossly offensive is a necessary measure for an actionable communication to be established. Yet, despite this, the level of offensiveness and the intended distress are insufficient to render an offence here on the same scale as harassment or stalking. Beyond that, the CPS has made it clear that social media offences will only be pursued where there is a public interest to do so.[174] This is not a social media specific test – but given the high threshold that must be met to satisfy the s1 requirements,[175] it imposes an additional – often impossible to satisfy – barrier to prosecution. It is more confusing that the requirements are so difficult to satisfy given that issues such as using false social media accounts to

170 CPS, 'Social Media – Guidelines on Prosecuting Cases Involving Communications Sent via Social Media' (*Crown Prosecution Service*, revised 21 August 2018) <www.cps.gov.uk/legal-guidance/social-media-guidelines-prosecuting-cases-involving-communications-sent-social-media> accessed 10 September 2018, para 14. There are some similarities in this requirement to the requirements which are present under the PHA 1997 in respect of harassment and stalking.

171 MCA 1988, s 4(a).

172 CPS, 'Social Media – Guidelines on Prosecuting Cases Involving Communications Sent via Social Media' (*Crown Prosecution Service*, revised 21 August 2018) <www.cps.gov.uk/legal-guidance/social-media-guidelines-prosecuting-cases-involving-communications-sent-social-media> accessed 10 September 2018, para 54.

173 See, for example, discussions above at 3.5. Stalking.

174 See 'Public Interest Stage of the Code for Prosecutors' in CPS, 'Social Media – Guidelines on Prosecuting Cases Involving Communications Sent via Social Media' (*Crown Prosecution Service*, revised 21 August 2018) <www.cps.gov.uk/legal-guidance/social-media-guidelines-prosecuting-cases-involving-communications-sent-social-media> accessed 10 September 2018.

175 Sarah Birkbeck, 'Can the Use of Social Media be Regulated?' (2013) 19 CTLR 83, 85.

threaten minors into producing and sharing intimate images – as was the situation in *R* v *Bradburn*[176] – can also be dealt with under this legislation. Simply because a prosecution for a social media offence is more challenging on an evidential basis,[177] does not mean that it ought to be brushed aside. Geach and Haralambous question whether there is any need for specific criminal offences dealing with – as they refer to it "online harassment."[178] The debate since such a question was initially posed has never really been settled – and remains ongoing.[179] What is increasingly apparent is that, despite hints of reform, the means of committing potentially criminal activities online have changed and the law – at least in this area – takes Raz's notion of relative stability[180] to an extreme. There is a pressing need for change in this area as s1 of the MCA is only partially suited to dealing with social media abuse.

Whilst some amendments have been forthcoming, these have predominantly focussed on alterations to sentencing under the MCA. The Criminal Justice and Courts Act introduced increased sentences for s1 offences[181] so that a higher maximum sentence could be imposed. This is undoubtedly a positive step – and a small indicator that there is an increased awareness of the inadequacies of the law in this area. The amendment also resulted in some – albeit limited – recognition that society – and technology – is changing behaviours but that the law is too often stagnant. Jeremy Wright MP made this point quite clearly: "the world is changing and we must change with it. We must recognise that the Internet and mobile phones are increasingly used to send or attempt to send offensive and distressing material (. . .) tough penalties should be available to the courts."[182] Unfortunately, such recognition has – in the four years since this statement – not been acted on further.

176 *R v Bradburn* [2017] EWCA Crim 1399.

177 CPS, 'Social Media – Guidelines on Prosecuting Cases Involving Communications Sent via Social Media' (*Crown Prosecution Service*, revised 21 August 2018) <www.cps.gov.uk/legal-guidance/social-media-guidelines-prosecuting-cases-involving-communications-sent-social-media> accessed 10 September 2018, paras 27–28.

178 Neal Geach and Nicola Haralambous, 'Regulating Harassment: Is the Law Fit for the Social Networking Age?' (2009) 73 JCL 241, 245.

179 Law Commission 'Offensive Online Communications: Current Project Status' (*Law Commission*, 5 February 2018) <www.lawcom.gov.uk/project/offensive-online-communications/> accessed 10 September 2018.

180 Joseph Raz, 'The Rule of Law and its Virtue' [1977] 93 LQR 195, 199.

181 CJCA 2015, s 32.

182 Criminal Justice and Courts Bill 2014, HC Deb 27 March 2014, col 493 (Jeremy Wright MP).

The second of the communications offences which can be utilised – depending on the circumstances of a particular case – is found within the CA 2003. The specific provisions within s127 introduce two criminal offences. First, where a person sends messages via a public electronic communications network that are "grossly offensive, or of an indecent, obscene or menacing character."[183] Second, where a person sends messages through a public electronic communications network messages that have as their purpose the causing of "annoyance, inconvenience or needless anxiety to another" and which are false,[184] or makes persistent use of a communications network to send messages to annoy, inconvenience, or cause anxiety.[185] The s127(2)(c) offence is the one which encapsulates the vast majority of low-level trolling activities on social media platforms, but there are low prosecution numbers because of the high public interest requirements which have to be satisfied.[186]

Where a successful prosecution is made, the maximum sentence available is one of six months in custody.[187] The sentencing level reflects the fact that the activity being addressed through s127 is not that which has an impact as such on the victim, rather it is the actions amounting to misuse of a public network which are the focus of the section. Moreover, where communications are sent privately, even if they meet the requirements of being grossly offensive, or are intended to cause anxiety, annoyance or inconvenience, they will not be pursued under s127 because there must be a public element to the communication. In such situations, the only prosecutorial option is to pursue a s1 MCA case.

The offences outlined in s127 require "grossly offensive" communications. This phrase – whilst differing from the phrases used in other legislation addressing substantive offences – replicates the test in s1(a)(ii) MCA. It is therefore the essence of making a successful case on the basis of communications misuse, and yet, despite its longevity in legislation – from 1988 to 2018 – remains controversial and difficult to precisely define.[188] This is especially the situation given the perilous nature of criminalising speech[189] and it

183 CA 2003, s 127(1)(a).
184 ibid, s 127(2)(a).
185 ibid, s 127(2)(c).
186 Birkbeck, 'Can the Use of Social Media Be Regulated?' (n 175) 85.
187 CA 2003, s 127(3).
188 No definition appears in the legislation.
189 Birkbeck, 'Can the Use of Social Media Be Regulated?' (n 175) 84.

is therefore critical to note that s127 – and s1 – do not criminalise speech per se. Rather, they criminalise the manner in which that speech reaches its audience and impose consequences for speech which is deemed to be damaging by the judicial system. Despite the controversy, these provisions – limited though they are – serve as reminders that (1) there are consequences for actions online and (2) the Internet is not an unregulated space. This is perhaps most apparent in that a prosecution under s127 requires simply that the message or communication is sent.[190] This has much broader coverage than the s1 MCA offence – for s127, 'sending' will also cover messages which are posted on a social media platform rather than those directly sent to the intended recipient. Significantly, s127 will also extend to reposts – or in a Twitter context, retweets and, as such, liability will still arise even if you were not the person who wrote the original message.[191]

Determining what is meant by "grossly offensive" within the context of a s127 communication is to be identified – according to Lord Bingham – by the context in the case:

> [t]here can be no yardstick of gross offensiveness otherwise than by the application of reasonably enlightened, but not perfectionist, contemporary standards to the particular message sent in its particular context. The test is whether a message is couched in terms liable to cause gross offence to those to whom it relates.[192]

Similarly, there must be an intention to cause significant offence to the people to whom the words relate.[193] In particular, if the words show a clear intent to cause offence, there is nothing else to consider.[194] Beyond this, where messages of a menacing character are considered under s127(b), this too will be dependent on the objective question of fact in the specific circumstances of the case.[195] This is the reality of the

190 CPS, 'Social Media – Guidelines on Prosecuting Cases Involving Communications Sent via Social Media' (*Crown Prosecution Service*, revised 21 August 2018) <www.cps.gov.uk/legal-guidance/social-media-guidelines-prosecuting-cases-involving-communications-sent-social-media> accessed 10 September 2018, para 14.

191 A point Sally Bercow learnt the hard way in *McAlpine v Bercow* [2013] EWHC 1342 (QB).

192 *Collins v DPP* [2006] UKHL 40 [9] (Lord Bingham).

193 *Sweet v Parsley* [1970] AC 132.

194 ibid, 148 (Lord Reid).

195 *Chambers* (n 39); *Karsten v Wood Green Crown Court* [2014] EWHC 2900 (Admin) (per Laws LJ).

assessments to be made under s127 – specifically because to be more stringent and prescriptive in setting the limitations would risk accidental criminalisation of speech. The approach adopted by the courts to interpreting what is meant by grossly offensive and menacing, is required because whilst some speech is undeniably unpalatable, that alone does not mean that the speech is also criminal – a balancing act therefore has to be cautiously managed in the opinion of Laws LJ[196] and Mr Justice Sweeney.[197]

In essence, whilst s127 is not a perfect statutory section, it is the most modern iteration of the statutory prohibitions on public nuisance committed in the specific confines of public communications networks.[198] Such nuisances – whilst suggestive again of trivialities – are expressly prohibited by statute,[199] even if the statute is far from a perfect fit for the newer types of nuisance.

S1 MCA is the only communications offence available where the communication is not sent via a public network. This is problematic where the communications are sent directly but privately to the victims, for example sending a direct message to another user on Twitter. An offence under s1 will still potentially be prosecutable but few other offences will be available for consideration. This very much places the burden of dealing with communications misuse on two statutory sections, and two alone. More problematically, the s127 offence is regarded by the CPS as the default and, whilst it operates at a lower threshold than s1 MCA, s127 has also been held out as having a threshold which is too high and too strict to allow for convictions to be pursued.[200] As such, given the type of behaviour – and the impact inflicted on the victims – in question, the legal system makes it very difficult to prove prosecutions for instances of social media abuse, especially where that abuse may be serious.

Discussions of provisions designed to tackle threats, abusive behaviour, harassment, and stalking have shown that much of the existing legislation is not suited to dealing with social media abuse. In addition, where some provisions could be suited to doing so,

196 *Karsten*, ibid [21].

197 *Smith* (n 50) [34].

198 *Chambers* (n 39).

199 *R v Rimmington* [2005] UKHL 63 [29] (Lord Bingham).

200 Council of Europe Parliamentary Assembly Committee on Equality and Non-Discrimination, 'Ending Cyberdiscrimination and Online Hate, Report by Rapporteur Marit Maij' (n 6) para 32.

barriers are in place to prevent this being effective. Having only two provisions – both of which have very high evidential thresholds and both of which frequently see cases fail to meet the public interest test for prosecution – is an indicator that social media abuse gets only scant attention from the justice system. The attitude towards prosecutions, in particular from the CPS, is suggestive of social media problems being dismissed – even in 2018 – as trivial or frivolous. Finally, all of this leads to a lack of cohesion – and ultimately, something of a dismissive attitude towards pernicious harms disregarded by evidential and prosecutorial thresholds that are too high to satisfy.

3.8 Conclusions

The legislative landscape – in terms of both substantive criminal provisions and communications provisions – lacks clarity. The range of offences, some of which could be utilised to deal with social media abuse where it reaches a criminal threshold, all refer to different behaviours. Beyond this, whilst the behaviours and evidential thresholds are all distinct from one another, the terminology used is not. This indicates not only a lack of clarity within the law as a whole, but also a lack of understanding of the subtle distinctions in behaviour which can have different, and devastating, impacts on victims. An analysis of the provisions indicates that the focus within the existing legislation is not on the right elements – the emphasis ought to rest on the impact of the behaviour complained of, rather than elements such as 'proximity' or 'hearing.' In short, the regulatory regime is a failure in this area and still focuses on means of abuse such as envelopes rather than the words transmitted. Furthermore, abuse committed by images is recognised as a behaviour which should receive specific legal provisions – the same is not said for the graphical equivalents on social media. Finally, the distinction – and a stark one – drawn by the CPS between 'substantive' criminal offences and offences under the communications provisions summarises neatly the basic problem in this area: that social media abuse – particularly that targeted towards women – is not taken seriously, nor is the harm it causes recognised by the organs of the judicial system. This further evidences the continuing gender-bias of the law – where the law fails to tackle these issues, it becomes complicit in reinforcing these gendered forms of abusive and – frequently – violent behaviours.

Bibliography

Table of cases

England & Wales
Atkin v DPP [1989] Crim LR 581
C v CPS [2008] EWHC 148 (Admin)
Calland v FCA [2015] EWCA Civ 192
Campbell v Mirror Group Newspapers [2004] UKHL 22
Chambers v DPP [2012] EWHC 2157 (Admin)
Chambers and Edwards v DPP [1995] Crim LR 896
Chappell v DPP (1989) Cr 82
Collins v DPP [2006] UKHL 40
Colman v Godwin (1783) 3 Doug KB 90
Conn v Sunderland City Council [2007] EWCA Civ 1492
Connolly v DPP [2007] EWHC 237 (Admin)
Dhir v Saddler [2017] EWHC 3155 QB
Dowson v Chief Constable of Northumbria Police [2010] EWHC 2612 (QB)
DPP v Orum [1989] 1 WLR 88
DPP v Smith [2017] EWHC 3193 (Admin)
Ferguson v British Gas Trading Ltd [2009] EWCA Civ 46
Gough v DPP [2013] EWHC 3267 (Admin)
Harvey v DPP [2011] EWHC 3992 (Admin), [2012] Crim LR 553
James v DPP [2009] EWHC 2925 (Admin)
Karsten v Wood Green Crown Court [2014] EWHC 2900 (Admin)
Lau v DPP [2000] 1 FLR 799
Levi v Bates [2015] EWCA Civ 206
Majrowski v Guy's and St Thomas' NHS Trust [2005] EWCA Civ 251
McAlpine v Bercow [2013] EWHC 1342 (QB)
Pratt v DPP [2001] EWHC Admin 483
R v Bradburn [2017] EWCA Crim 1399
R v Curtis [2010] EWCA Crim 123
R v Danevska [2017] EWCA Crim 1084
R v Haque [2011] EWCA Crim 1871
R v Henley [2000] Crim LR 582 CA (Crim Div)
R v Nimmo & Sorley (Westminster Magistrates' Court, 24 January 2014)
R v Patel [2005] 1 Cr App R 27
R v Peter's [2002] EWCA Crim 1721
R v Qosja [2016] EWCA Crim 1543
R v Rimmington [2005] UKHL 63
R v Sheppard [2010] EWCA Crim 65, [2010] 1 WLR 2779
R v Smith (Mark) [2012] EWCA Crim 2566
R v Tan [2017] EWCA Crim 493
R v Viscount St Davids (Westminster Magistrates' Court, 11 July 2017)
R v Widdows [2011] EWCA Crim 1500
R (A Child) v DPP [2001] EWHC 17 (Admin)

R (Hogle) v DPP [2015] ACD 84
S v DPP [2008] EWHC 438 (Admin)
Southard v DPP [2006] EWHC 3449 (Admin)
Sweet v Parsley [1970] AC 132
Taylor v DPP [2006] EWHC 1202 (Admin)
Thomas v News Group Newspapers Ltd [2001] EWCA Civ 1235

European Court of Human Rights
Delfi AS v Estonia App no 64569/09 (ECtHR, 16 June 2015)

Table of legislation (UK and EU) and regional treaties

UK Public General Acts
Communications Act 2003
Crime and Courts Act 2013
Criminal Law Act 1977
Criminal Justice and Courts Act 2015
Criminal Justice and Public Order Act 1994
Malicious Communications Act 1988
Offences Against the Person Act 1861
Policing and Crime Act 2017
Protection from Harassment Act 1997
Protection of Freedoms Act 2012
Public Order Act 1986
Scotland Act 1998
Serious Organised Crime and Police Act 2005

Acts of the Scottish Parliament
Criminal Justice and Licensing Act (Scotland) 2010 (asp 13)

European Union Legislation
Directive 2000/31/EC of the European Parliament and of the Council of 8 June 2000 on Certain Legal Aspects of Information Society Services, in Particular Electronic Commerce, in the Internal Market ('Directive on Electronic Commerce') [2000] OJ L178/1

Regional Treaties
Convention for the Protection of Human Rights and Fundamental Freedoms (European Convention on Human Rights, as amended) (ECHR)

List of Secondary Sources

Contributions to Edited Books
Barker K, 'R v Nimmo and Sorley [2014]' in Rackley E and Auchmuty R (eds), *Women's Legal Landmarks: Celebrating 100 Years of Women and Law in the UK and Ireland* (Hart Publishing, 2018)
—and Jurasz O, 'Gender, Human Rights and Cybercrime: Are Virtual Worlds Really That Different?' in Asimow M, Brown K and Papke DR (eds), *Law and Popular Culture: International Perspectives* (Cambridge Scholars Publishing 2014)

Crown Prosecution Service Guidelines

CPS, 'Social Media – Guidelines on Prosecuting Cases Involving Communications Sent via Social Media' (*Crown Prosecution Service*, revised 21 August 2018) <www.cps.gov.uk/legal-guidance/social-media-guidelines-prosecuting-cases-involving-communications-sent-social-media> accessed 10 September 2018

CPS, 'Stalking and Harassment' (*Crown Prosecution Service*, last updated 23 May 2018) <www.cps.gov.uk/legal-guidance/stalking-and-harassment> accessed 10 September 2018

Council of Europe Reports

Council of Europe Parliamentary Assembly Committee on Equality and Non-Discrimination, 'Ending Cyberdiscrimination and Online Hate, Report by Rapporteur Marit Maij' (13 December 2016) Doc 14217 <http://semantic-pace.net/tools/pdf.aspx?doc=aHR0cDovL2Fzc2VtYmx5LmNvZS5pbnQvbncveG1sL1hSZWYvWDJILURXLWV4dHIuYXNwP2ZpbGVpZD0yMzIzNCZsYW5nPUVO&xsl=aHR0cDovL3NlbWFudGljcGFjZS5uZXQvWHNsdC9QZGYvWFJlZi1XRC1BVC1YTUwyUERGLnhzbA==&xsltparams=ZmlsZWlkPTIzMjM0> accessed 10 September 2018

European Union Publications

Commission, 'European Commission and IT Companies Announce Code of Conduct on Illegal Online Hate Speech' (Press Release, Brussels, 31 May 2016) <http://europa.eu/rapid/press-release_IP-16-1937_en.htm> accessed 10 September 2018

Evidence Submissions

Barker K and Jurasz O, 'Submission of Evidence to Scottish Government Independent Review of Hate Crime Legislation (Bracadale Review)' (*Open University*, December 2017) <http://oro.open.ac.uk/52612/> accessed 10 September 2018

Explanatory Notes to Statutes

Explanatory Notes to the Protection for Freedoms Act 2012

Explanatory Notes to the Serious Organised Crime and Police Act 2005

Governmental Notices and Publications

Home Office, 'Circular: A Change to the Protection from Harassment Act 1997' (HM Government, Home Office Circular 018/2012, 16 October 2012) <www.gov.uk/government/publications/a-change-to-the-protection-from-harassment-act-1997-introduction-of-two-new-specific-offences-of-stalking> accessed 10 September 2018

Hansard

HC Deb 27 March 2014, col 493

HL Deb 24 January 1997, vol 577, cols 918–920

House of Commons Bills

Criminal Justice and Courts Bill 2014

House of Commons Library Publications

Strickland P and Douse D, '"Insulting Words or Behaviour": Section 5 of the Public Order Act 1986' (*House of Commons Library*, Commons Briefing Paper SN05760, 15 January 2013) <https://researchbriefings.parliament.uk/ResearchBriefing/Summary/SN05760#fullreport> accessed 10 September 2018

Journal Articles

Agate J and Ledward J, 'Social Media: How the Net is Closing in on Cyber Bullies' (2013) *24 EntLR* 263

Birkbeck S, 'Can the Use of Social Media be Regulated?' (2013) *19 CTLR* 83

Geach N and Haralambous N, 'Regulating Harassment: Is the Law Fit for the Social Networking Age?' (2009) *73 JCL* 241

Leggatt Z, 'Now or Never? How Imminent Must a Fear of Violence Be for the Purposes of s 4A of the Protection from Harassment Act 1997? R v Qosja (Robert)' (2017) *81 JCL* 17

MacEwan N, 'The New Stalking Offences in English law: Will They Provide Effective Protection from Cyberstalking?' [2012] *10 Crim LR* 767

McGlynn C and Rackley E, 'Image-Based Sexual Abuse' (2017) *37 OJLS* 534

Newman C, 'Offensive Picture on the Internet Later Shown to Complainant by a Third Party Causing Distress' (2008) *72 JCL* 481

Ormerod D, 'Case Comment: *James v DPP:* Harassment – Appellant Phoning Social Services – Victim Not Available to Take Appellant's Calls – Victim Later Returning Phone Calls' (2010) *7 Crim LR* 580

Raz J, 'The Rule of Law and its Virtue' [1977] *93 LQR* 195

Spitzberg BH and Cupach WR, 'The State of the Art of Stalking: Taking Stock of the Emerging Literature' (2007) *12 Aggression and Violent Behaviour* 64

Taylor N, 'Gough (Stephen Peter) v Director of Public Prosecutions: Public Order – Appellant Walking Nude through a Town Centre. Divisional Court; PQBD Sir Brian Leveson and Openshaw J: October 31; [2013] EWHC 3267 (Admin)' (2014) *5 Crim LR* 371

Willcox R, '*Levi v Bates* – Harassment and the Concept of Targeted Behaviour' (2015) *26 EntLR* 209

Newspaper Articles

Cooper Y, 'Why I'm Campaigning to Reclaim the Internet from Sexist Trolls' *The Telegraph* (London, 26 May 2016) <www.telegraph.co.uk/women/politics/why-im-campaigning-to-reclaim-the-internet-from-sexist-trolls/> accessed 10 September 2018

Parliamentary Reports

Communications Select Committee, *Social Media and Criminal Offences* (HL 2014–15, 37)

Websites

Amnesty International, 'Toxic Twitter – A Toxic Place for Women' (*Amnesty International*, 2018) <www.amnesty.org/en/latest/research/2018/03/online-violence-against-women-chapter-1/> accessed 10 September 2018

Braithwaite P, 'Smart Home Tech Is Being Turned into a Tool for Domestic Abuse' (*Wired*, 22 July 2018) <www.wired.co.uk/article/internet-of-things-smart-home-domestic-abuse> accessed 10 September 2018

Everyday Sexism Project <https://everydaysexism.com> accessed 10 September 2018.

Glitch!UK <https://seyiakiwowo.com/GlitchUK/> accessed 10 September 2018

Law Commission 'Offensive Online Communications: Current Project Status' (*Law Commission*, 5 February 2018) <www.lawcom.gov.uk/project/offensive-online-communications/> accessed 10 September 2018

Leitão R, 'When Smart Homes Become Smart Prisons' (*DigiCult*) <https://digicult.it/news/when-smart-homes-become-smart-prisons/#_edn1> accessed 10 September 2018

Reclaim the Internet <http://www.reclaimtheinternet.com> accessed 10 September 2018

Suzy Lamplugh Trust, 'Managing Stalking Offenders' (*Suzy Lamplugh Trust*) <www.suzylamplugh.org/managing-stalking-offenders> accessed 10 September 2018

4 Hate crime

The limits of the law

> Online hate is a reflection of hate in our societies. It is crucial therefore that strategies to eliminate hate in the online environment acknowledge and tackle the hatred and intolerance in people's hearts and minds.
>
> COE, 2017.[1]

4.1 Introduction

In addressing online hate as well as its gendered aspects, this book advances the position that the law is in the need of reform so as to offer a route of redress for sufferers of online abuse. Specifically, it is argued that online misogyny must be viewed as a form of hate crime in order to give long overdue recognition to the fact that gender-based hate is equally serious to hate based on other, protected, characteristics. However, in making this proposal, this chapter identifies the existing limitations embedded in the hate crime framework in England & Wales which applies to instances of online hate generally and online misogyny specifically. It is proposed that in order to address online misogyny within the framework of hate crime, two steps need to be taken. First, a long-overdue recognition of the fact that gender (and not only sexual orientation or transgender identity) can be a ground for hate, prejudice or bias which motivates commission of a criminal offence. Second, and in parallel to adding gender as a protected characteristic, it is proposed that specific offences dealing with online social media abuse are created.

As highlighted in Chapter 1, law reform is not the only solution to resolving the problem of widespread (online) misogyny and (online) hate in today's society. The issue is much more complex and deeply

1 Council of Europe, 'Ending Cyberdiscrimination and Online Hate' (CoE Res 2144, text adopted 25 January 2017), para 4.

DOI: 10.4324/9780429956805-4

rooted in the structural hierarchies as well as reflective of the social attitudes and stereotypes represented in modern society.[2] Reducing this issue to a one-dimensional legal perspective would only significantly underestimate these complexities further. Nonetheless, the law has played (and, as it is argued in this book, should play) a role in combatting hate crime, including its gendered and online forms. Importantly, law reform should aim to reflect the contemporary nature of hate crimes being committed online and also rectify its long-standing gender bias which is represented in the exclusion of "gender" as a protected characteristic. Crucially, these steps would not only bring the legislative hate crime framework in England & Wales into the twenty-first century but also offer more meaningful avenues of redress to the victims of gender-based online hate crimes.

4.2 Hate crime: development and classifications

Hate crime laws have largely developed in the second-half of the twentieth century, although violence motivated by hate or bias has been occurring for centuries. In Europe, the creation of hate crime laws can be observed in the interwar period, but was significantly heightened in the aftermath of World War II, which was marked by the rise of racist and nationalistic laws and policies as well as the tragic atrocities of the Holocaust. It is therefore unsurprising that in years following the end of World War II, which coincided with the period of rapid decolonisation and the rise of apartheid policies, many European states enacted laws prohibiting and punishing acts motivated by racial hate or bias.[3] However, the hate crime framework as we know it today in England & Wales developed largely in the last 30 years,[4] although the offence of

2 See generally Mark A Walters, Rupert Brown and Susann Wiedlitzka, *Research Report 102: Causes and Motivations of Hate Crime* (Equality and Human Rights Commission, July 2016) <www.equalityhumanrights.com/sites/default/files/research-report-102-causes-and-motivations-of-hate-crime.pdf> accessed 10 September 2018, 25–41. See further discussions on attitudes in Chapter 2, 2.2. Social media abuse as a modern phenomenon.

3 For an overview of the development of anti-hate laws in Germany, France and Britain, see Erik Bleich, 'From Race to Hate: *A Historical Perspective*' in Thomas Brudholm and Birgitte Schepelern Johansen (eds), *Hate, Politics, Law: Critical Perspectives on Combatting Hate* (OUP 2018) 16–20.

4 For a comprehensive overview of the historical development of hate crime legislation in England & Wales see: Law Commission, *Hate Crime: The Case for Extending the Existing Offences* (Law Com CP No 213, 2013) app B (History of Hate Crime Legislation).

stirring up racial hatred was previously enacted in the Race Relations Act 1965.[5]

The attempts by states to combat anti-Semitism and racism through domestic legislation have also been accompanied by legal developments at an international level. Concerns about the pressing need to tackle hate have been central to the post-war era and are reflected in the anti-discrimination provisions enshrined in the United Nations human rights treaties. For example, the International Convention on Elimination of All Forms of Racial Discrimination 1965 (ICERD) makes explicit reference to the prohibition of discrimination, including on grounds of "race, colour, descent, or national or ethnic origin"[6] and places an obligation on state parties to the convention to create laws prohibiting and punishing "dissemination of ideas based on racial superiority or hatred as well as acts of violence or incitement to such acts against any race or group of persons of another colour or ethnic origin."[7] In addition, the International Covenant on Civil and Political Rights 1966 states that "[a]ny advocacy of national, racial or religious hatred that constitutes incitement to discrimination, hostility or violence should be prohibited by law."[8] However, despite the general prohibition of discrimination in international human rights law (including on grounds of sex/gender) there exist no equivalent provisions aiming to prohibit advocacy of gender-based hatred or prejudice that constitutes incitement to discrimination, hostility or violence.[9]

Examination of the early developments of hate crime laws prompts two observations. First, there is a notable absence of the notion of sex and/or gender-based hostility or bias in the early legislation concerning hate. Given the historical, as well as socio-cultural, context at the time the absence of considerations of "gender" is notable, although not unique to the issue of hate, prejudice or bias based on this

5 Race Relations Act 1965, s 6.

6 International Convention on the Elimination of All Forms of Racial Discrimination (opened for signature 21 December 1965, entered into force 4 January 1969) 660 UNTS 212 (ICERD), art 1(1).

7 ibid, art 4(a).

8 International Covenant on Civil and Political Rights (adopted 16 December 1966, entered into force 23 March 1976) 999 UNTS 171 (ICCPR), art 20.

9 This includes the Convention on the Elimination of All Forms of Discrimination Against Women 1979 which is the key UN treaty specifically addressing discrimination against women – see Convention on the Elimination of All Forms of Discrimination Against Women (adopted 18 December 1979, entered into force 3 September 1981) 1249 UNTS 13 (CEDAW).

characteristic. Rather, it is an example of the (too) long tradition of ignoring gender in the legal context as well as maintaining or creating laws which discriminate against women based on their gender.[10] In many respects, parallels can be drawn here with the absence of consideration of prejudice or bias towards persons identifying as LGBTQI in the early hate crime legislation. Nonetheless, these parallels no longer apply when considering later developments in hate crime legislation. For instance, in England & Wales, prejudice or bias based on sexual orientation or transgender identity were included in the legislation as early as 1986 and 2003 respectively,[11] whereas prejudice or bias based on gender alone (rather than transgender identity or sexual orientation) is still awaiting its legal recognition as "worthy" of protecting against. At present, gender does not feature as a protected characteristic under the laws of England & Wales, nor is there an aggravated offence based on gender-based prejudice or bias.[12]

Second, it can be observed that the development of hate crime laws has typically been incentivised by the occurrence of tragic, extremely violent or otherwise "unthinkable" events which shock the conscience. For instance, the centrality of racial, nationalistic, and religious prejudice and discrimination to the atrocities committed during World War II was reflected in the enactment of anti-hate laws in Europe in the post-war period. Likewise, Chakraborti and Garland observe that high profile cases such as the racist murder of black teenager Stephen Lawrence in 1993, as well as the racist and homophobic nail bomb attacks carried out by the neo-Nazi David Copeland in London in 1999, have led to a significant rise in the currency of the term hate crime and, what follows, the legal response to this phenomenon.[13] At the same time, such tragic events often lead to a rise in hate crime (e.g. in

10 See generally, Joanne Conaghan, *Law and Gender* (OUP, 2013). For example, it was only in the late 1960s and early 1970s that Equal Pay Acts were adopted in the US (Equal Pay Act of 1963, 29 USC § 206(d)) and in the UK (Equal Pay Act 1970). Also, in the 1960s there was no universal suffrage in many countries across the globe. For example, women gained a right to vote in Switzerland as late as 1971.

11 Public Order Act 1986, pt 3A; Criminal Justice Act 2003, s 146 (transgender identity and sexual orientation); Criminal Justice (Scotland) Act 2003 (asp 7), s 2(3) (transgender identity and sexual orientation).

12 Kim Barker and Olga Jurasz, 'Submission of Evidence to Scottish Government Independent Review of Hate Crime Legislation (Bracadale Review)' (*Open University*, December 2017) <http://oro.open.ac.uk/52612/> accessed 10 September 2018.

13 Neil Chakraborti and Jon Garland, *Hate Crime: Impact, Causes & Responses* (2nd edn, SAGE 2015) 1–2.

the aftermath of 9/11 attacks and London 7/7 bombings) and calls for strengthening the existing hate crime laws.[14]

These are, of course, valid motivations and rationales for creating, amending, and implementing hate crime laws. However, they do raise the question of why gender as a characteristic has been continuously absent from the hate crime framework in England & Wales despite the prevalence of various forms of gender-based violence against women, in both public and private spheres. It is equally concerning that tragic and violent events, as well as high profile cases involving hateful and threatening behaviours and/or messages being directed at women due to gender-based prejudice or bias, have not resulted in the incorporation of gender as a protected characteristic in hate crime laws in England & Wales, and in Scotland. On the contrary, gender-based aspects of such acts are frequently absent from the public narrative concerning a given case (as, for instance, in the case of the murder of Labour MP Jo Cox[15]). The discrepancy between the effects of tragic events motivated by gender-based prejudice or bias vis-*à*-vis the effect of events motivated by other (protected) characteristics is not only striking but also indicative of the manner in which gender-based hate, prejudice or bias is ultimately tolerated within society and within the legal system of England & Wales. Furthermore, they evidence how gender-based violence, misogyny and gender-based prejudice have become normalised[16] in modern times to the extent that, despite their widespread and "everyday" occurrence, they are perceived as falling outside the scope of the legal regulation of hate crime.

Building on these initial observations, this chapter will examine the position of gender within the context of online hate crime, specifically misogynistic text-based abuse, and contrast it with the existing legal framework on hate crime in England & Wales. Furthermore, drawing on recent developments, this chapter will make a case for adding gender to the current list of protected characteristics. It will also make proposals for legislative steps which ought to be taken in order for the legal system to enable prosecution of online, misogynistic, text-based abuse as a hate crime.

14 For instance, in March 2018, the All Party Parliamentary Group on Hate Crime launched an inquiry into hate crime entitled "How do we build community cohesion when hate crime is on the rise?" about which see APPG, 'Inquiries' (*APPG Hate Crime*, 2018) <www.appghatecrime.org/inquiries/> accessed 10 September 2018.

15 See discussions in Chapter 2, 2.3. From offline to online: the digital misogyny 'switch.'

16 ibid.

4.2.1 Defining hate crime

There exists a breadth of definitions of hate crime which contributes to the complexity of addressing this issue – not least from a legal perspective.[17] Whilst sharing some common characteristics (such as a focus on hostility, prejudice or bias against specific groups in society, or violence, or threat[18] of violence directed against member(s) of these groups), these definitions understandably, and for good reason, vary depending on the academic discipline from which they stem, as well as the purpose for which they are conceived. It is then not surprising to observe that legislative definitions which set out the requirements that need to be satisfied for a criminal conviction are narrower than, for example, definitions proposed by scholars in sociology or criminology.[19] For instance, the police in England & Wales and the Crown Prosecution Service (CPS) have agreed the following definition for identifying and flagging hate crimes:

> Any criminal offence which is perceived by the victim or any other person, to be motivated by hostility or prejudice, based on a person's disability or perceived disability; race or perceived race; or religion or perceived religion; or sexual orientation or perceived sexual orientation or transgender identity or perceived transgender identity.[20]

In contrast, the definition proposed by Barbara Perry acknowledges the conceptual complexity of hate crime and draws on its relationship to structural hierarchies existing in society:

> Hate crime (. . .) involves acts of violence and intimidation, usually directed towards already stigmatised and marginalised groups.

17 Definitional ambiguity is further reflected in varying definitions of hate crime proposed by the institutions working at a supranational level. See generally, Jon Garland and Neil Chakraborti, 'Divided by a Common Concept: Assessing the Implications of Different Conceptualisations of Hate Crime in the European Union' (2012) 9 EJC 38.

18 See further discussions relating to the Public Order Act in Chapter 3, 3.4. Threats and threats to kill.

19 Barbara Perry, *In the Name of Hate: Understanding Hate Crimes* (Routledge 2001); Paul Iganski, '*Hate Crime*' *and the City* (The Policy Press 2008); Barbara Perry, 'The Sociology of Hate: Theoretical Approaches' in Brian Levin (ed), *Hate Crimes: Understanding and Defining Hate Crime* (Praeger Publications, 2009); Nathan Hall, *Hate Crime* (2nd edn, Routledge 2013).

20 CPS, 'Hate Crime' (*Crown Prosecution Service*, 2017) <www.cps.gov.uk/hate-crime> accessed 10 September 2018.

> As such, it is a mechanism of power and oppression, intended to reaffirm the precarious hierarchies that characterise a given social order. It attempts to re-create simultaneously the threatened (real or imagined) hegemony of the perpetrator's group and the 'appropriate' subordinate identity of the victim's group. It is a means of marking both the Self and the Other in such a way as to re-establish their 'proper' relative positions, as given and reproduced by broader ideologies and patterns of social and political inequality.[21]

Perry's definition, which has gained the strongest support from criminologists working in the field of hate crime,[22] highlights the multiple factors that inform our understanding of hate crime. By placing the definition within the social context, Perry emphasises the power dynamics which underscore the commission of hate crimes and which are reflected in the "hegemony of the perpetrator's group and the 'appropriate' subordinate identity of the victim's group."[23]

The additional difficulty associated with defining hate crime is due to the perceived subjectivity of hate. As Chakraborti and Garland note, the

> "emotive and conceptually ambiguous label of hate (. . .) has important implications for the way in which we conceive of the offences that fall under its umbrella framework and of the actors involved in a hate crime, whether these be victims, perpetrators, or criminal justice and other organisations."[24]

This has a direct correlation to the ways in which hate crimes are positioned within the existing legislation as well as to the manner in which hate crimes are recorded – and prosecuted. Subjective perceptions of hate also feed into the controversial nature of hate crime, particularly with regard to which characteristics are protected and, therefore, legally recognised as more "deserving" of greater punishment than offences driven by hostility, bias, or prejudice based on other factors. This in itself raises a deeper, and perhaps even more contested, question of the hierarchy of harms resulting from crimes motivated by the

21 Perry, *In the Name of Hate* (n 19) 10.

22 Chakraborti and Garland also note that Perry's definition of hate crime has gained the strongest support from criminologists working in the field of hate crime: Neil Chakraborti and Jon Garland, 'Hate Crime' in Walter S DeKeseredy and Molly Dragiewicz (eds), *Routledge Handbook of Critical Criminology* (Routledge 2011) 304.

23 Perry, *In the Name of Hate* (n 19) 10.

24 Chakraborti and Garland, *Hate Crime* (n 13) 2.

five officially recognised categories of hate crimes vis-*à*-vis crimes motivated by prejudice based on unprotected characteristics.

4.2.2 Hate crime v hate speech

Hate crime and hate speech are closely related and are often used interchangeably, despite significant conceptual differences. In short, the underlying conduct in hate crime is already criminal (i.e. an offence existing in criminal law has been committed), with hate against a member (or members) of a specific group constituting an accompanying motive. It is the latter factor that makes the crime in question a "hate crime." In contrast, the content of hate speech expresses, promotes, incites, encourages or stirs-up hatred towards a person or persons due to their characteristic feature(s) – for instance, such as race, nationality or sexual orientation. "Hatred," Waldron notes, "is relevant [here] not as the motivation of certain actions, but as a possible effect of certain forms of speech."[25] This distinction between hate speech and hate crime is crucial as not every act of (online) hate speech would become an (online) hate crime, unless an existing criminal offence has been committed through the act of (online) hate speech *and* is motivated by hate, prejudice, or bias related to one of the five (currently) protected characteristics in sections 145 and 146 of the Criminal Justice Act 2003.

Similar to hate crime, there exists no universally agreed definition of hate speech. Most states and organisations, as well as social media platforms, adopt their own definitions of hate speech and this compounds the difficulties in distinguishing between speech and crime. In its 2015 General Policy Recommendation No.15 on combatting hate speech, the European Commission against Racism and Intolerance (ECRI) of the Council of Europe proposed a broad definition of hate speech:

> Hate speech is to be understood (. . .) as the advocacy, promotion or incitement, in any form, of the denigration, hatred or vilification of a person or group of persons, as well as any harassment, insult, negative stereotyping, stigmatization or threat in respect of such a person or group of persons and the justification of all the preceding types of expression, on the ground of 'race', colour, descent, national or ethnic origin, age, disability, language,

25 Jeremy Waldron, *The Harm in Hate Speech* (Harvard University Press 2012) 35.

> religion or belief, sex, gender, gender identity, sexual orientation and other personal characteristics or status. [H]ate speech may take the form of the public denial, trivialisation, justification or condonation of crimes of genocide, crimes against humanity or war crimes which have been found by courts to have occurred, and of the glorification of persons convicted for having committed such crimes.[26]

Finally, various social media platforms employ varying definitions of hate speech as well as demonstrating various degrees of restrictions with regard to prohibiting hate speech and/or removing hateful content. For instance, Facebook community standards refer directly to the removal of hate speech, which is understood as: "content that directly attacks people based on their race, ethnicity, national origin, religious affiliation, sexual orientation, sex, gender or gender identity or serious disabilities or diseases."[27] In addition, organisations and people who are dedicated to "promoting hatred against these protected groups are not allowed a presence on Facebook."[28]

In contrast, Twitter's Terms of Service do not explicitly prohibit hate speech on its platform – rather, users are forewarned that they "may be exposed to Content that might be offensive, harmful, inaccurate or otherwise inappropriate."[29] Furthermore, Twitter clarifies that the sole responsibility for content is borne by the person who originated it: "We may not monitor or control the Content posted via the Services and, we cannot take responsibility for such Content."

The position of Twitter on the issue is particularly curious given the recent reports concerning the volume and impact of gender-based abuse perpetrated on the platform.[30] Furthermore, it stands in stark contrast to the Council of Europe's approach which calls for

26 European Commission against Racism and Intolerance, ECRI General Policy Recommendation No 15 on Combatting Hate Speech (Council of Europe, adopted 8 December 2015) <https://rm.coe.int/ecri-general-policy-recommendation-no-15-on-combating-hate-speech/16808b5b01> accessed 10 September 2018.

27 Facebook, 'Community Standards' (*Facebook*, 2018) <www.facebook.com/communitystandards/hate_speech> accessed 10 September 2018.

28 ibid.

29 Twitter, 'Twitter Terms of Service' (*Twitter*, effective 25 May 2018) <https://twitter.com/en/tos#intlTerms> accessed 10 September 2018.

30 Amnesty International, 'Toxic Twitter – A Toxic Place for Women' (*Amnesty International*, 2018) <www.amnesty.org/en/latest/research/2018/03/online-violence-against-women-chapter-1/> accessed 10 September 2018.

greater regulation concerning online hate, including its gender-based manifestations.[31]

4.2.3 Hate speech and human rights

Legal regulation of hate speech has proven controversial in a human rights context as it is directly counterbalanced by the protections concerning freedom of expression enshrined in Article 10 of the European Convention on Human Rights as well as other international instruments.[32] For example, whilst the European Court of Human Rights notes that:

> Freedom of expression constitutes one of the essential foundations of [a democratic] society, (. . .) it is applicable not only to 'information' or 'ideas' that are favourably received or regarded as inoffensive or as a matter of indifference, but also to those that offend, shock or disturb the State or any sector of the population[33]

it also remarks that:

> [T]olerance and respect for the equal dignity of all human beings constitute the foundations of a democratic, pluralistic society. That being so, as a matter of principle it may be considered necessary in certain democratic societies to sanction or even prevent all forms of expression which spread, incite, promote or justify hatred based on intolerance.[34]

The Court also clarified that incitement to hatred can take various forms, which do not necessarily need to expressly call for an act of violence to be committed. In *Vejdeland v Sweden*, the first decision

31 Council of Europe, 'Ending Cyberdiscrimination and Online Hate' (n 1).
32 Convention on the Prevention and Punishment of the Crime of Genocide (adopted 9 December 1948, entered into force 12 January 1951) 1021 UNTS 278 (Genocide Convention), art III(c) ("direct and public incitement to commit genocide"); ICCPR 1966, arts 19 and 20 (respectively, freedom of expression (including permissible grounds for restricting the right) and advocacy of national, racial or religious hatred that constitutes incitement to discrimination, hostility or violence); ICERD, arts 4 and 5 (all dissemination of ideas based on racial superiority or racial hatred, incitement to racial discrimination, with due regard to the right to freedom of expression).
33 *Handyside v UK* App no 5493/72 (ECtHR, 7 December 1976), para 49.
34 *Erbakan v Turkey* App no 59405/00 (ECtHR, 6 July 2006), para 56.

where the ECtHR applied the principles relating to hate speech in the context of sexual orientation, the Court emphasised that:

> inciting to hatred does not necessarily entail a call for an act of violence, or other criminal acts. Attacks on persons committed by insulting, holding up to ridicule or slandering specific groups of the population can be sufficient for the authorities to favour combating racist speech in the face of freedom of expression exercised in an irresponsible manner.[35]

Striking the balance between ensuring the freedom of expression rights and protection from hate speech (which stands in opposition to other core values in a democratic society, such as equality, tolerance, and prohibition of non-discrimination), continues to be challenging. Furthermore, the emergence of forms of hate speech in online environments – for example, through online, misogynistic text-based abuse as explored in this book – make it a pressing issue to address from both a policy and a law-making perspective.[36]

In *Delfi v Estonia*, the ECtHR was confronted with the issue of online hate speech in considering the liability of one of Estonia's largest online news portals (Delfi) for the offensive comments posted by one of its readers below one of the online news articles it hosted. In confirming that that Estonian courts' finding of liability against Delfi had been a justified and proportionate restriction on the news portal's freedom of expression, the Grand Chamber reasoned that:

> where third-party user comments are in the form of hate speech and direct threats to the physical integrity of individuals, as understood in the Court's case-law (. . .), the Court considers (. . .) that the rights and interests of others and of society as a whole may entitle Contracting States to impose liability on Internet news portals, without contravening Article 10 of the Convention, if they fail to take measures to remove clearly unlawful comments without delay, even without notice from the alleged victim or from third parties.[37]

35 *Vejdeland v Sweden* App no 1813/07 (ECtHR, 9 February 2012), para 54.
36 Dulcie Lee, Francis Elliott and Frances Gibb, 'MPs to Vote on Making Misogyny a Hate Crime in Legal First' *The Times* (London, 4 September 2018) <www.thetimes.co.uk/article/mps-to-vote-on-making-misogyny-a-hate-crime-in-legal-first-3qpwl766p> accessed 10 September 2018.
37 *Delfi AS v Estonia* App no 64569/09 (ECtHR, 16 June 2015), para 159.

The heavily criticised[38] finding in *Delfi* highlights the difficulties facing the courts when deciding on qualifications of online hate speech alongside defining the scope and the boundaries of the duties and responsibilities of the online platform providers. This can be particularly problematic where the Court goes beyond Article 12 of the EC Directive – and arguably Article 15 – by seeking to negate the so-called liability shield and impose a monitoring obligation on Internet Service Providers as a means to reduce their own liabilities. However, whilst the ECtHR has (thus far) not heard any cases concerning misogynistic (online) hate speech or cases concerning incitement to violence against women, the Council of Europe *has* emphasised the importance of addressing sexist (online) hate speech. Preventing and combatting (online) sexist hate speech has been framed as a strategic objective within the Gender Equality Strategy since 2014.[39] It is recognised that such steps are crucial to combat gender stereotyping and gender discrimination,[40] and prevent the (online) incitement of violence against women,[41] but also to ensure equal participation of women in the public sphere.[42]

However, despite these developments at a supranational level, the current hate crime framework in England & Wales, and in Scotland, is inadequately equipped to address the issue of online (as well as offline) misogyny, especially when it takes the form of gender-based, misogynistic text-based abuse. Building on the critique of the legal framework outlined in Chapter 3, the next section explores the current boundaries and shortcomings in the existing legal framework concerning hate crime in England & Wales.

38 Dirk Voorhoof, 'Qualification of News Portal as Publisher of Users' Comment May Have Far-Reaching Consequences for Online Freedom of Expression: Delfi AS v. Estonia' (*Strasbourg Observers*, 25 October 2013) <https://strasbourgobservers.com/2013/10/25/qualification-of-news-portal-as-publisher-of-users-comment-may-have-far-reaching-consequences-for-online-freedom-of-expression-delfi-as-v-estonia/> accessed 10 September 2018.

39 Council of Europe, *Council of Europe Gender Equality Strategy 2014–2017* (Council of Europe, February 2014) <https://rm.coe.int/1680590174> accessed 10 September 2018, 9–10; Council of Europe, *Council of Europe Gender Equality Strategy 2018–2023* (Council of Europe, June 2018) <https://rm.coe.int/prems-093618-gbr-gender-equality-strategy-2023-web-a5/16808b47e1> accessed 10 September 2018, paras 19, 40, 44.

40 Council of Europe, *Council of Europe Gender Equality Strategy 2014-2017*, ibid.

41 Council of Europe, 'Ending Cyberdiscrimination and Online Hate' (n 1), para 7.2.2.

42 Council of Europe, 'Ending Cyberdiscrimination and Online Hate' (n 1); Council of Europe, 'Putting an End to Sexual Violence and Harassment of Women in Public Space' (CoE Res 2177, text adopted 29 June 2017).

4.2.4 Hate crime: the current legal framework in England & Wales

The current legal framework in England & Wales represents a threefold approach to punishing hate crime: first, through aggravated offences; second, through offences of 'stirring up hatred,' and third, through provisions allowing for enhanced sentencing.

Aggravated offences are contained in ss 28–32 of the Crime and Disorder Act 1998.[43] Under the CDA, if a person commits one of the offences listed in ss 29–32 and, in doing so, demonstrates, or was motivated by, hostility on the grounds of race or religion, that offence becomes a separate "aggravated" offence, with a higher sentencing tariff available. Importantly, the CDA 1998 provisions allow for the imposition of higher sentences for aggravated offences based on race or religion only. At present, the aggravated offences under the law of England & Wales do not cover hostility based on the remaining three protected characteristics: sexual orientation, transgender identity or disability. This in itself is already demonstrative of the unequal treatment of the protected characteristics under hate crime legislation, giving (once again) rise to a hierarchy of harms suffered by the victims. The Law Commission reflected on this undesirable state of the law in 2014 noting that:

> [i]t sends the wrong message about the seriousness with which such offending is taken and the severity of its impact, if offences attaching a specific aggravated label and a potentially higher sentence only exist in relation to two of the five statutorily protected hate crime characteristics.[44]

The second category of hate crime offences is the offences concerning "stirring up hatred" which are enshrined in the Public Order Act 1986 (POA 1986). Whilst these provisions allow for the prosecution of persons who stir up hatred on grounds of race (Part 3 of POA), religion or sexual orientation (Part 3A of POA), the current stirring up offences do not cover hatred on grounds of transgender identity or disability.

In addition to the aggravated offences and stirring up offences, the law in England & Wales provides for special, enhanced sentencing powers in successful prosecutions of hate crimes. These are set out in

43 Hereafter, CDA 1998.

44 Law Commission, *Hate Crime: Should the Current Offences be Extended?* (Law Com No 348, 2014) 12.

ss 145 and 146 of the Criminal Justice Act 2003[45] which allow the judge to increase the sentence for an offender convicted of any offence,[46] if it was motivated by hostility or involved a demonstration of hostility on the basis of any of the five protected characteristics: race, religion, sexual orientation, transgender identity or disability.[47]

4.2.5 Who is protected against hate crime?

Protected characteristics are the core part of the legal framework on hate crime. They identify specific features which motivate hostility or prejudice leading to the commission of a criminal offence which ultimately becomes a hate crime. The characteristics currently protected under the law in England & Wales are race, religion, sexual orientation, disability, and transgender identity.

Although hate crimes in England & Wales are recorded for all five of these protected characteristics, the criminal offences that specifically deal with hate crime only cover some of the characteristics. This unequal focus within the legislation has rightfully invited criticism – from academics, practitioners, third sector organisations, and law-making bodies alike – expressing concerns related to the discriminatory aspects of the current approach to protected characteristics within the legal framework on hate crime.[48] For example, the 2014 Law Commission report on hate crime revealed a notable level of inequality within the existing legal provisions concerning protected characteristics whereby race and religion appear to be afforded much greater protection than sexual orientation, disability, and transgender identity.[49] This is due to the fact that these two characteristics are included in all the provisions dealing with hate crime, i.e. aggravated offences, stirring up offences as well as enhanced sentencing, whereas the

45 Hereafter, CJA 2003.

46 With exception of offences already covered by CDA 1998, ss 29–32 (see CJA 2003, s 145(3)).

47 The test for the demonstration or motivation of hostility is the same as that used in the aggravated offences provisions. For a comprehensive overview of the tests, see Law Commission, *Hate Crime: Should the Current Offences be Extended?* (n 44).

48 ibid; Gail Mason, 'Victim Attributes in Hate Crime Law: Difference and Politics of Justice' (2014) 54 BritJCriminol 161; Chara Bakalis, 'The Victims of Hate Crime and the Principles of the Criminal Law' (2017) 37 LS 718; Barker and Jurasz, *Submission of Evidence to Scottish Government Independent Review of Hate Crime Legislation (Bracadale Review)* (n 12).

49 Law Commission, *Hate Crime: Should the Current Offences be Extended?* (n 44) 83 – 85.

remaining three characteristics are only eligible for enhanced sentencing under the CJA 2003 (with the exception of sexual orientation which is also included in the context of the stirring up offences in POA 1986).

This disparity in the treatment of protected characteristics within laws on hate crime raises doubts about the perceived impact of such offending and the seriousness with which it is taken by the legal system. Furthermore, it leads to the creation of a "hierarchy of harms"[50] within the hate crime framework where victimisation arising from certain protected characteristics (race, religion) supersedes harms sustained by victims of crimes motivated by hostility or bias based on sexual orientation, disability and/or transgender identity.

However, this inconsistent approach to protection also raises a broader – and highlights an underlying – question of why certain characteristics are protected by law and others are not.[51] The literature on hate crime and practice from various jurisdictions[52] indicates diverse approaches to a) why certain groups should be protected due to their special/distinctive characteristics and b) which characteristics ought to be protected. The determination of these two issues reflects a difficult and controversial process as it, ultimately, makes a statement as to which social groups in society are worthy of higher protection by law than others. In acknowledging this legal challenge, Schweppe notes that these distinctions have an impact on victims and offenders alike:

> By singling out specific groups, the legislature is sending a clear message that these groups are deserving of more protection than others. This means that the legislature is classifying distinct victim types as more worthy of legal protection – legal protection which has an enormous impact on the offender during the sentencing stage. When the legislature chooses to discriminate between offenders, placing certain offenders into a category, any offence against which automatically requires an enhanced sentence, it

50 For more on this point, see Chapter 2.

51 Generally, there exists a lack of consensus on the issue of protected characteristics across the EU. See generally Garland and Chakraborti, 'Divided by a common concept' (n 17).

52 For an overview of protected characteristics in other selected jurisdictions, see James Chalmers and Fiona Leverick, *A Comparative Analysis of Hate Crime Legislation: A Report to the Hate Crime Legislation Review* (Scottish Government, July 2017) <https://consult.gov.scot/hate-crime/independent-review-of-hate-crime-legislation/supporting_documents/495517_APPENDIX%20%20ACADEMIC%20REPORT.pdf> accessed 10 September 2018, 52–57.

must do so carefully, and with the principle of equality for offenders and victims in mind.[53]

How, then, it is decided which characteristics get protected within the legal system and which do not? The literature points towards a plethora of approaches which, very much like the definition of hate crime, depend on the specific focus of the discipline from which a given approach emerges. For instance, Chakraborti and Garland advocate for an approach based on perceived vulnerability and difference, which "would acknowledge that *all* vulnerable communities and social groups, irrespective of minority or majority status, can be the subject of hate crime, and that this violence can have a devastating effect."[54] This approach, whilst attractive in its conceptual and open-ended domain, can nonetheless be criticised for potentially perpetuating a perception of hate crime victims as powerless and weak. When considered from a gender perspective, this could be considered a significant flaw, resulting in the creation of a false image of women exclusively through the lens of their perceived vulnerability, weakness, and subordination.

Other authors have suggested approaches based on a group identity where members of a given group share common characteristics (or self-identify as a group),[55] as well as argued for protection based on immutability of the characteristic(s). Both approaches have been largely contested[56] – in the case of the former, for being potentially both over and under inclusive and, in the case of the latter, for creating a legally unacceptable situation whereby victims with immutable characteristics are perceived to be more worthy of protection that victims whose characteristics can change.

However, one of the most mainstream approaches towards determination of protected characteristics is based on the notion of historical disadvantage or, following Reidy, "long lasting, historical, group-based oppression."[57] This approach places the notion of his-

53 Jennifer Schweppe, 'Defining Characteristics and Politicizing Victims: A Legal Perspective' (2012) 10 Journal of Hate Studies 173, 187.

54 Garland and Chakraborti, 'Divided by a common concept' (n 17) 49.

55 Frederick M Lawrence, *Punishing Hate: Bias Crimes under American Law* (Harvard University Press 1999) 12.

56 Alexander Brown, 'The 'Who' Question in the Hate Speech Debate: Part 1: Consistency, Practical, and Formal Approaches' (2016) 29 CJLJ 275, 303; Schweppe, 'Defining Characteristics and Politicizing Victims' (n 53) 179–83.

57 OSCE, *Hate Crime Laws: A Practical Guide* (OSCE Office for Democratic Institutions and Human Rights (ODIHR) 2009) <www.osce.org/odihr/36426?download=true>

torically conditioned oppression or discrimination of a given group at its centre, pointing towards a long-standing inequality which was a direct result of the aforementioned factors. Arguments based on the historical inequality approach have been advanced in the context of "offline" and "online" hate crime alike – including in favour of combatting various forms of discrimination online. For instance, Daniels emphasises "collective awareness of historical inequality"[58] in a call for greater regulation of cyber racism. As such, Daniels emphasised that what may be perceived as a "historical inequality" also characterises contemporary interactions between people in the online domain in the very same vein as misogyny which has spanned offline and online environments.[59]

Jenness and Grattet also note the centrality of violence, or threat of violence, in maintaining such inequality,[60] whilst Reidy draws attention to the role of states and/or governments in upholding the unequal status of a given group:

> long lasting historical, group-based oppression is rarely accomplished without significant state or governmental action. Thus, where a particular disproportionate vulnerability, or, more likely, a general pattern of such vulnerabilities, arises out of historical oppression, there are good reasons to think that the state or government, in addition to citizens collectively, has a special obligation to respond.[61]

The "historical inequality/disadvantage" approach therefore makes a strong and straightforward case for the inclusion of gender amongst other protected characteristics. For centuries, women have been forced into positions of inequality in comparison to men. Such positions have not only been maintained by various states/governments (not least including the jurisdictions covered in this book) but also reinforced by the creation and enforcement of laws which place women in a socially and legally inferior position to men. Furthermore, such

accessed 10 September 2018, 38; David A Reidy, 'Hate Crimes, Oppression and Legal Theory' (2002) 16 Public Affairs Quarterly 259, 275.

58 Jessie Daniels, *Cyber Racism: White Supremacy Online and the New Attack on Civil Rights* (Rowman & Littlefield Publishers 2009) 24.

59 For a fuller discussion of online misogyny, see Chapter 2.

60 Valerie Jenness and Ryken Grattet, *Making Hate A Crime: From Social Movement to Law Enforcement* (Russell Sage Foundation 2001) 122.

61 Reidy, 'Hate Crimes, Oppression and Legal Theory' (n 57) 275.

laws legitimise various forms of gender-based violence against women and have supported women's inequality in multiple contexts, such as civil and political rights, property ownership and rights, and private and public gender-based violence. Ironically, there is arguably a notion of universality in this "historical inequality" in that it was not specific to only some jurisdictions or certain geographical regions. Rather, this unequal status has been (and sadly, in many cases, continues to be) experienced by women worldwide and is often found to be further exacerbated by other, intersecting characteristics.[62] Writing in 1995, Choundas aptly summarised this ironic status quo:

> despite their status-created vulnerability to the same patterns of discriminatory violence experienced by other groups, women are, nevertheless, not considered 'equal' to other hate crime victims in terms of the seriousness and urgency of the harm inflicted, and the 'protection of the laws,' in the most literal and immediate sense, is arbitrarily denied them.[63]

Nearly 25 years on, Choundas' reflection is still current. Therefore, it is even more astonishing that the addition of gender as a protected characteristic under hate crime laws continues to be a controversial, or at least highly disputed proposal. On balance, given its long-standing role in maintaining the inequality of women, the law has a role to play in redressing imbalances in the context of hate crime.

4.3 Extending the boundaries of hate crime: hate (re)defined

Although the previous sections of this chapter may give an impression that the boundaries of hate crime are strictly fixed, this is certainly not the case. The issue of reform of hate crime laws in England & Wales was taken up by the Law Commission in 2013, while the Independent Review of Hate Crime Legislation in Scotland was undertaken by Lord Bracadale in 2017.[64] Most recently, as a result of the vote on the

62 See below at 4.3.1. *Why the need to include gender in hate crime laws?*

63 George P Choundas, 'Neither Equal nor Protected: The Invisible Law of Equal Protection, the Legal Invisibility of its Gender-Based Victims' (1995) 44 Emory LJ 1069, 1072.

64 Law Commission, *Hate Crime: Should the Current Offences be Extended?* (n 44); Scottish Government, *Independent Review of Hate Crime Legislation in Scotland: Consultation Paper* (Scottish Government, August 2017) <www.gov.scot/Resource/0052/

amendment to the Voyeurism (Offences) Bill, the Government committed to carrying out a full review into all hate crime law, including misogyny[65] with the Scottish Government announcing intent to consult on hate crime in 2018–19.[66] Whilst neither review has yet resulted in any substantive changes in legislation, they represent, nonetheless, a fair indicator that uncertainties exist about the current state of legislation in this area as well as its suitability – especially with regard to protected characteristics.

Whilst any change in legislation is certainly a complex (and therefore likely time-consuming) task, other indicators of a change in the approach towards hate crime can be observed. One particular area in which such changes are notable is the manner in which hate crimes are flagged by police forces. Despite the fact that current legislation focuses strictly on five protected characteristics, the police can in fact "flag" other crimes as hate crimes even where the basis for prejudice or bias is not legislated for. According to the guidance issued by the College of Policing in 2014, the five currently protected and monitored strands of hate crime "are the minimum categories that police officers and staff are expected to record," allowing forces to record other forms of hostility and prejudice.[67] Generally, this approach has emerged in recognition of the crimes which are motivated by hate, prejudice or bias against identifiable groups of people but not legally identified as a protected for purposes of monitoring and punishing hate crime.[68] It is additionally influenced by consideration of a noticeable pattern of crimes against certain groups in certain communities (e.g. violent attacks on the street sex workers in Merseyside) or as a response to tragic – and often high-profile – events (e.g. the death of Sophie Lancaster leading to the monitoring of subculture hate crime by

00524055.pdf> accessed 10 September 2018 (Bracadale Review); Scottish Government, *Independent Review of Hate Crime Legislation in Scotland: Final Report* (Scottish Government, May 2018) <www.gov.scot/Resource/0053/00535892.pdf> accessed 10 September 2018 (Bracadale Review: Final Report).

65 Libby Brooks, 'Review Brings Misogyny as a Hate Crime a Step Closer' *The Guardian* (London, 6 September 2018) <www.theguardian.com/society/2018/sep/05/first-step-to-misogyny-becoming-a-hate-called-amazing-victory> accessed 10 September 2018.

66 Scottish Government, *Delivering for Today, Investing for Tomorrow: The Government's Programme for Scotland 2018–19* (Scottish Government, September 2018) <www.gov.scot/Resource/0053/00539972.pdf> accessed 10 September 2018.

67 College of Policing, *Hate Crime Operational Guidance* (College of Policing, May 2014) <www.college.police.uk/What-we-do/Support/Equality/Documents/Hate-Crime-Operational-Guidance.pdf> accessed 10 September 2018, 7.

68 ibid.

Greater Manchester Police in 2013).[69] As such, the police are allowed a degree of flexibility in shifting the existing conceptual boundaries of hate crime in response to changes in social attitudes towards certain groups/characteristics, although it is worth noting that the flagging of such offences would not result in prosecution of the offence as a hate crime due to the lack of legislative basis for it. Indeed, this flexibility has been exercised by some police forces in England to record instances of gender hate crime[70] and misogyny hate crime,[71] thereby supporting the view that law is in need of reform to reflect the harmful nature of gender-based hate, prejudice or bias. Whilst this may be seen as a positive development, the flagging of gender-based hate alone will not bring the required change, particularly where it comes to providing remedies to the victims of such crimes and holding perpetrators accountable. It is therefore hard to be optimistic about such developments, despite common assessments of them as "victories" – particularly by third sector organisations.

The following sections present compelling arguments and justification for extending the existing boundaries of hate crime by including gender as a protected characteristic in England & Wales, and in Scotland. Building on this proposal and examining the specificity of online hate, it is then argued that the law ought to address a specific and gender-based form of online hate – online misogyny – as a hate crime.

4.3.1 Why the need to include gender in hate crime laws?

Suggestions for the inclusion of gender as a protected characteristic are not new. In fact, American scholars highlighted this issue in the

69 ibid, 8.

70 Esme Ashcroft, 'Cat-Calling and Wolf-Whistling Now Classed as Gender-Hate Crimes by Avon and Somerset Police' *Bristol Post* (Bristol, 16 October 2017) <www.bristolpost.co.uk/news/bristol-news/gender-hate-now-recognised-crime-635194?utm_content=bufferf8757&utm_medium=social&utm_source=twitter.com&utm_campaign=buffer> accessed 10 September 2018.

71 Mark Townsend, 'Police in England and Wales Consider Making Misogyny a Hate Crime' *The Guardian* (London, 10 September 2016) <www.theguardian.com/society/2016/sep/10/misogyny-hate-crime-nottingham-police-crackdown> accessed 10 September 2018. See also: Nottinghamshire Police, 'Hate Crime' (*Nottinghamshire Police*, 2018) <www.nottinghamshire.police.uk/hatecrime> accessed 10 September 2018; North Yorkshire Police, 'Misogyny to be Recognised as a Hate Crime from Wednesday 10 May 2017' (*North Yorkshire Police*, 10 May 2017) <https://northyorkshire.police.uk/news/misogyny-recognised-hate-crime-wednesday-10-may-2017/> accessed 10 September 2018.

early 1990s, pointing towards the lack of parity between gender and other characteristics protected under hate crime statutes in the United States.[72] More recently, calls for the incorporation of gender within the list of protected characteristics in relation to hate crime laws have been made in the UK[73] as well as in Australia and New Zealand,[74] with many authors directly viewing gender-based hostility, prejudice or bias as a motivation for gender-based violence against women. For instance, Maher *et al.* emphasise the symbolic value of using aggravated sentencing in cases involving gender-based hate crime: not only to "illuminate systematic and underpinning social attitudes in relation to everyday violence against women" but also "for gendered hate to become more visible, more readily contested and, ultimately, less acceptable."[75]

However, the exclusion of gender from the list of protected characteristics has practical implications – not only from the perspective of punishment and redress but also for the way in which hate crime is conceptualised and understood. In particular, it results in the production of an incomplete picture and knowledge concerning hate crime and its gender dimension. Through the elimination of gender-based hostility, prejudice or bias from hate crime legislation, hate victimisation of women due to their gender is effectively "stricken off the record," making the gender aspect of hate crime effectively invisible – both in hate crime discourse and in practice. It also obscures the complexity of hate crime and its intersectionality.[76] Whilst the legal system

72 Marguerite Angelari, 'Hate Crime Statutes: A Promising Tool for Fighting Violence Against Women' (1994) 2 AmUJGender & L 63; Steven Bennett Weisburd and Brian Levin, 'On the Basis of Sex: Recognizing Gender-Based Bias Crimes' (1994) 5 Stan L & Pol'y Rev 21; Choundas, 'Neither Equal nor Protected' (n 63).

73 Hannah Mason-Bish and Aisha K Gill, 'Addressing Violence Against Women as a Form of Hate Crime: Limitations and Possibilities' (2013) 105 Feminist Review 1; Mark A Walters and Jessica Tumath, 'Gender 'Hostility', Rape, and the Hate Crime Paradigm' (2014) 77 MLR 563

74 Charlotte Brown, 'Legislating Against Hate Crime in New Zealand: The Need to Recognise Gender-Based Violence' (2004) 35 VUWLR 591; Kylie Weston-Scheuber, 'Gender and the Prohibition of Hate Speech' (2012) 12 QUT Law & Justice Journal 132; Jane Maree Maher, Jude McCulloch and Gail Mason, 'Punishing Gendered Violence as Hate Crime: Aggravated Sentences as a Means of Recognising Hate as Motivation for Violent Crimes Against Women' (2015) 41 AFLJ 177.

75 Maher, McCulloch and Mason, 'Punishing Gendered Violence as Hate Crime', ibid, 192–93.

76 For a discussion of intersectionality and hate crime, see Hannah Mason-Bish, 'Beyond the Silo: Rethinking Hate Crime and Intersectionality' in Nathan Hall and others (eds), *The Routledge International Handbook on Hate Crime* (Routledge 2014).

recognises that hate crime can be motivated by more than one characteristic (amongst those legally "protected"), it does not acknowledge that gender plays an equally significant role in the perpetration of hate crimes which are so deeply influenced by the societal, cultural, and structural factors.[77] This gap is nonetheless created despite the general acknowledgement of gender as a factor shaping everyday lives and a factor recognised in other branches of the law as a ground on which differential and discriminatory treatment frequently occurs.

Instead, the current law appears to favour a simple (if not simplistic) approach to formulating the victim's identity in the context of hate crime. It turns a blind eye to the variety of characteristics (outside those already deemed as "protected") which contribute to the complex nature of the identity of many of the hate crime victims, which ultimately is a key factor in the commission of a hate crime. As such, the law ignores "the differences, the heterogeneity, within what are assumed to be homogenous identity categories and groups."[78] The absence of a gender perspective from hate crime discourse is already affecting the way in which hate incidents motivated by gender-based hostility, prejudice or bias (either as a sole factor or one of multiple factors) are spoken about, perceived, and reported in the media. For instance, the well documented volume of online abuse received by Labour MP, Diane Abbott, was almost universally described as hateful.[79] However, Abbott's abuse was perceived to be solely motivated by her racial background,[80] rather than by hostility, prejudice or bias due to her overlapping identities (i.e. race *and* gender) as a black *and* female politician. Abbott herself recognised the multifaceted nature of the online abuse directed at her by publicly emphasising that the abuse she received was both racist and sexist.[81] Speaking in a parliamentary debate in 2017 about "mindless, racist and sexist" abuse she

77 See above at 4.2. Hate crime: development and classifications.

78 Leslie J Moran and Andrew N Sharpe, 'Violence, Identity and Policing: The Case of Violence Against Transgender People' (2004) 4 Criminal Justice 395, 400.

79 Azmina Dhrodia, 'Unsocial Media: Tracking Twitter Abuse against Women MPs' (*Medium*, 3 September 2017) <https://medium.com/@AmnestyInsights/unsocial-media-tracking-twitter-abuse-against-women-mps-fc28aeca498a> accessed 10 September 2018.

80 The abuse of Gina Miller (explored in Chapter 2, 2.3.3. *Intersectional abuse – still misogyny, still a techlash?*) was assessed in a similarly limited manner.

81 Rachel Sylvester and Alice Thomson, 'Diane Abbott Interview: 'Why Am I Abused So Much? I'm Both Black and a Woman'' *The Times* (London, 28 April 2018) <www.thetimes.co.uk/article/diane-abbott-saturday-interview-why-am-i-abused-so-much-i-m-both-black-and-a-woman-fd2vhdrc5> accessed 10 September 2018.

had been receiving, Abbott also challenged the salient misperception that online abuse directed at her (as well as against women generally) was happening as a "one off" occurrence or something characteristic to election time only, stressing the everyday, pervasive nature of such attacks.[82] However, the law continues to lag behind social realities and ignores calls for such recognition by the victims themselves.

4.3.2 Gender as a protected characteristic: towards law reform

The review of the hate crime framework in England & Wales through a gender lens confirms the pressing need for a greater legal recognition that hate, prejudice, or bias can be based on gender. As argued, there are multiple shortcomings in the current legislative landscape which have significant implications for the victims of gender-based hate crime. When considered from a legal standpoint, the current approach is particularly concerning from the perspective of equality legislation, which provides a much broader list of relevant protected characteristics. The principle of equality, the importance of which was referred to by Schweppe,[83] does not appear to be the determinant for the existing distinctions. The currently protected five characteristics do not fully reflect the characteristics protected in the core piece of equality legislation in the UK, The Equality Act 2010, which covers nine protected characteristics on the basis of which discrimination may occur.[84]

In order to redress this manifest inequality gap within the legal framework on hate crime, it is proposed that adding gender as a protected characteristic under hate crime legislation in England & Wales is a legislative priority.[85] This proposal resonates with the later recommendation of the Bracadale Review to amend hate crime legislation in Scotland by a) creating a new statutory aggravation based on

82 HC Deb 12 July 2017, vol 627, cols 159–60.

83 For more discussion of this, see above at 4.2.5. *Who is protected against hate crime?*

84 Equality Act 2010, s 4 (age, disability, gender reassignment, marriage and civil partnership, pregnancy and maternity, race, religion or belief, sex, sexual orientation). See also Bakalis, 'The Victims of Hate Crime and the Principles of the Criminal Law' (n 48).

85 Barker and Jurasz, *Submission of Evidence to Scottish Government Independent Review of Hate Crime Legislation (Bracadale Review)* (n 12); John Boothman, 'Academics Tell Bracadale Review: Make Online Misogynistic Abuse a Hate Crime' *The Times* (London, 8 April 2018) <www.thetimes.co.uk/article/academics-tell-bracadale-review-make-online-misogynistic-abuse-a-hate-crime-lfqcx2jt7> accessed 10 September 2018.

gender hostility[86] and b) introducing stirring up offences in respect of each protected characteristic, including any new protected characteristics.[87] The Report also recognises that adding such a type of aggravation to the hate crime legislation would also assist in the forming of an effective system to prosecute online hate crime and hate speech.[88] As we have argued elsewhere,[89] and crucially for this study, such an addition is necessary in order to effectively address (online) misogyny within the frameworks of hate crime legislation.

Notwithstanding the significance of such legislative amendments, it is recognised that merely including gender as a protected characteristic would not (or at least not immediately) change the social attitudes, gender stereotypes, and structural factors underpinning the existence of gender-based hostility, prejudice or bias. However, adding gender to the list of protected characteristics would also have a significant symbolic dimension. It would signify the long-overdue legal recognition of harms directed at and suffered by women *because they are women*. Nonetheless, its impact would likely be broader than that: by including gender (rather than specifying "women"), the extended list of protected characteristics would allow for the inclusion of other examples of victimisation caused by offences motivated by a victim's gender – not only when a victim is female. At long last, it would also send a clear message that hostility, prejudice or bias based on a person's gender is not tolerated by law and will be punished accordingly.

4.4 Online hate (crimes)

In recent years, there has been increasing recognition of the fast-growing phenomenon and impact of online hate (referred to also as cyber hate[90] or digital hate[91]), both in the academic literature across

86 Bracadale Review: Final Report (n 64) Recommendation 9, vii.
87 ibid, Recommendation 13, viii.
88 ibid, Recommendation 17, ix.
89 Barker and Jurasz, *Submission of Evidence to Scottish Government Independent Review of Hate Crime Legislation (Bracadale Review)* (n 12); Kim Barker and Olga Jurasz, 'Online Misogyny as Hate Crime: Tweeting Sense, Slaying Trolls' (Society of Legal Scholars Conference, Dublin, September 2017).
90 Chara Bakalis, 'Regulating Hate Crime in the Digital Age' in Jennifer Schweppe and Mark Austin Walters (eds), *The Globalization of Hate: Internationalizing Hate Crime?* (OUP 2016) 263.
91 Danielle Keats Citron, *Hate Crimes in Cyberspace* (Harvard University Press 2014).

various disciplines,[92] and in law and policy contexts at domestic and supranational[93] levels. In particular, academic legal research has pointed towards pressing, yet complex, issues concerning legal regulation of online hate in light of the everyday, extensive use of the Internet in private and public life.[94] However, despite the recognition of the multifaceted issues arising from online hate, there are only a few examples of academic commentary concerning the interrelationship between online, gender-based hate and law, especially from the perspective of creating a comprehensive legal regulation not limited to a narrow or singular area of the law.[95]

The rise of public interest in online hate crime is reflected in the decision to monitor instances of online hate in statistics on hate crime.[96] In April 2015, police flagging of "online crime" was officially introduced in order to allow for monitoring of "cases where it is believed that an offence was committed, in full or in part, through a computer, computer network or other computer-enabled device."[97] The

92 For contributions from disciplines other than law, see, for example: Phyllis B Gerstenfeld, Diana R Grant and Chau-Pu Chiang, 'Hate Online: A Content Analysis of Extremist Internet Sites' (2003) 3 ASAP 29; Matthew Williams, *Virtually Criminal: Crime, Deviance and Regulation Online* (Routledge 2006); Karen M Douglas, 'Psychology, Discrimination and Hate Groups Online' in Adam Joinson and others (eds), *The Oxford Handbook of Internet Psychology* (OUP 2007); Bailey Poland, *Haters: Harassment, Abuse, and Violence Online* (University of Nebraska Press 2016).

93 Iginio Gagliardone and others, *Countering Online Hate Speech* (UNESCO 2015) <http://unesdoc.unesco.org/images/0023/002332/233231e.pdf> accessed 10 September 2018; Council of Europe, 'Ending Cyberdiscrimination and Online Hate' (n 1).

94 James Banks, 'Regulating Hate Speech Online' (2010) 24(3) IRLCT 233; Citron, *Hate Crimes in Cyberspace* (n 91); Bakalis, 'Regulating Hate Crime in the Digital Age' (n 90); Natalie Alkiviadou, 'Regulating Internet Hate: A Flying Pig?' (2016) 7 JIPITEC 216; Natalie Alkiviadou, 'Hate Speech on Social Media Networks: Towards a Regulatory Framework?' (2018) I& CTL (published online 4 July 2018) <https://doi.org/10.1080/13600834.2018.1494417> accessed 10 September 2018.

95 Kim Barker and Olga Jurasz, 'Submission of Evidence on Online Violence Against Women to the UN Special Rapporteur on Violence Against Women, its Causes and Consequences, Dr Dubravka Šimonović' (*Open University*, November 2017) <http://oro.open.ac.uk/52611/> accessed 10 September 2018; Barker and Jurasz, *Submission of Evidence to Scottish Government Independent Review of Hate Crime Legislation (Bracadale Review)* (n 12).

96 Yet, ironically, social media offences consistently fail to satisfy the public interest threshold required by the CPS to prosecute such offences – a point discussed at length in Chapter 3.

97 Aoife O'Neill, *Hate Crime, England and Wales, 2016/17* (Home Office, Statistical Bulletin 17/7, 10 October 2017) 18.

first statistics including an "online crime" flag showed that 2% (1067 offences) of all hate crimes reported in 2016–17 in England & Wales were committed online.[98] The results have demonstrated that race and sexual orientation were the top two motivating factors for online hate crimes.[99] As the statistics do not contain gender-disaggregated data, it is not possible to identify the gender of victims and/or perpetrators of these online hate crimes. Similarly, because gender is not a protected characteristic under the law of England & Wales, gender-motivated hate crime is not reflected in these statistics. This is despite the fact that some police forces in England have started to flag misogyny hate crimes and gender hate crimes.[100]

In August 2017, the Director of Public Prosecutions, Alison Saunders, expressed a public commitment to combatting online hate, especially on social media.[101] Saunders' announcement was welcome – not only due to the pressing need for the CPS to clamp down on online hate crime – but also because it gave explicit recognition to the harmful impact of online hate: "Whether shouted in their face on the street, daubed on their wall or tweeted into their living room, the impact of hateful abuse on a victim can be equally devastating."[102] However, Saunders' promise to "crack down" on social media crime has unsurprisingly raised questions concerning the resources available to the CPS to cope with the inevitable increase in demand for prosecutions. It also invited scepticism amongst lawyers who pointed out that the high evidential threshold test introduced by Saunders' predecessor, Keir Starmer, might hinder prosecution of social media hate crime cases.[103] Crucially, the increase in demand for prosecution has not

98 ibid.
99 ibid.
100 See above – 4.3. Extending the boundaries of hate crime: hate (re)defined.
101 Alison Saunders, 'Hate is Hate. Online Abusers Must Be Dealt with Harshly' *The Guardian* (London, 21 August 2017) <www.theguardian.com/commentisfree/2017/aug/20/hate-crimes-online-abusers-prosecutors-serious-crackdown-internet-face-to-face?utm_source=dlvr.it&utm_medium=twitter> accessed 10 September 2018.
102 Vikram Dodd, 'CPS to Crack Down on Social Media Hate Crime, Says Alison Saunders' *The Guardian* (London, 21 August 2017) <www.theguardian.com/society/2017/aug/21/cps-to-crack-down-on-social-media-hate-says-alison-saunders> accessed 10 September 2018.
103 ORG, 'ORG Response to CPS Announcement on Social Media Hate Crime' (*Open Rights Group*, 21 August 2017) <www.openrightsgroup.org/press/releases/2017/org-response-to-cps-announcement-on-social-media-hate-crime> accessed 10 September 2018. This point is specifically commented on by Ms Marit Maij, rapporteur to the Council of Europe Parliamentary Assembly Committee on

been reflected in the CPS's approach to the assessment of public interest in relation to offences committed via social media, including social media abuse, resulting in the scarcity of statistics.

Combatting online hate has also become a significant issue politically – in particular, after the announcement of the scale of online abuse of female politicians during the general election campaigns in 2017. This announcement raised concerns regarding intimidation of political candidates and the obstacles posed by online hate to the existence of democratic participation.[104] In April 2017, a new unit to tackle online hate crime in London, the Online Hate Crime Hub, was launched by the Mayor of London, Sadiq Khan.[105] Shortly after, in October 2017, the national equivalent of such an expert unit was announced by the (then) Home Secretary, Amber Rudd.[106] Nonetheless, despite making the headlines, none of these initiatives have addressed the gendered nature of online hate, nor have they assisted its victims.

However, it is hard not to be sceptical about the actual impact of such developments when considering them from a gender perspective. Whilst the UK Prime Minister, Theresa May, reflected on the online intimidation and online harassment of female politicians during her speech on the centenary of the 1918 Suffrage Act (Representation of People Act 1918), the "everyday" instances of online misogyny directed at women, as well as other instances of gendered online abuse,

---

Equality and Non-Discrimination, in her report: see Council of Europe Parliamentary Assembly Committee on Equality and Non-Discrimination, 'Ending Cyberdiscrimination and Online Hate, Report by Rapporteur Marit Maij' (13 December 2016) Doc 14217 <http://semantic-pace.net/tools/pdf.aspx?doc=aHR0cDovL2Fzc2VtYmx5LmNvZS5pbnQvbncveG1sL1hSZWYvWDJILURXLWV4dHIuYXNwP2ZpbGVpZD0yMzIzNCZsYW5nPUVO&xsl=aHR0cDovL3NlbWFudGljcGFjZS5uZXQvWHNsdC9QZGYvWFJlZi1XRC1BVC1YTUwyUERGLnhzbA==&xsltparams=ZmlsZWlkPTIzMjM0> accessed 10 September 2018, para 32.

104 Dhrodia, 'Unsocial Media' (n 79); Cabinet Office, *Protecting the Debate: Intimidation, Influence and Information* (HM Government, 29 July 2018) <https://assets.publishing.service.gov.uk/government/uploads/system/uploads/attachment_data/file/730209/CSPL.pdf> accessed 10 September 2018 (noting instances of intimidation of female politicians on the Internet).

105 Mayor of London, 'Mayor Launches New Unit to Tackle Online Hate Crime' (*Mayor of London and London Assembly*, 24 April 2017) <www.london.gov.uk/press-releases/mayoral/mayor-launches-unit-to-tackle-online-hate-crime> accessed 10 September 2018.

106 Home Office, 'Home Secretary Announces New National Online Hate Crime Hub' (*HM Government*, 8 October 2017) <www.gov.uk/government/news/home-secretary-announces-new-national-online-hate-crime-hub> accessed 10 September 2018.

remained outside the scope of the Prime Minister's remarks. What is more, little has changed in terms of the substantive law that deals with gender-motivated (online) hate and, especially, online misogyny. Whilst a decision to flag up gender hate crime and misogyny hate crime by a few police forces in England marks, at least symbolically, a step in the right direction, it has no implication for the higher sentencing tariffs for the perpetrators of such crimes. Also, as explored below, the current landscape dealing with (online) hate crime is overly complicated and does not adequately reflect the specificity of the environments in which online hate is perpetrated, nor does this address the gender dimension of such incidents. As such, the overall message sent through the legal system is one of ignorance of the long-term, large scale gendered harms resulting from (online) gendered hate and online misogyny which are deeply embedded in the structural discrimination against women and girls and reflective of the deeply entrenched gender stereotypes which permeate contemporary (digital) society.

4.4.1 Does online make it different?

The 2016 Equality and Human Rights Commission Report observed that the vast number of instances of online hate suggest that "those who feel prejudices towards certain protected characteristics are more likely to act online than offline."[107] Whilst this observation has not been confirmed by the official statistics of *reported* hate crimes in England & Wales in 2016–17,[108] the sheer scale of everyday occurrences of online hate *incidents* and online hate *speech* is alarming. It also shows that factors such as the perceived anonymity and invisibility of the perpetrator, the ease and speed with which online hate groups can assemble and target individuals or spread hateful content, and the instant, public, and wide-reaching nature of online communications on social media play a considerable role in the perpetration of online hate speech.[109] Because online hate speech carries these distinctive features, their specificity ought to inform the shaping of multi-faceted prevention and redress responses to this widespread problem. However, Brown argues that these distinctive features of online hate do not

107 Equality and Human Rights Commission, *Research Report 102: Causes and Motivations of Hate Crime* (n 2) 40.

108 See discussions below at 4.5. Online misogyny as a hate crime.

109 Citron, *Hate Crimes in Cyberspace* (n 91) 57–68; Council of Europe, 'Ending Cyberdiscrimination and Online Hate' (n 1), para 4.

necessarily warrant a different legal approach as far as criminal law is concerned:

> Nevertheless, it is not clear that this rapidity of change and the challenge of combating online hate speech by means of legislation and criminal prosecutions is significantly different for online as compared to offline hate speech. Hate speakers who prefer to do their hate speaking face-to-face can also exhibit ingenuity, creativity, playfulness, and innovation in content, and this too can pose a problem for legislators and legal professionals. Think of the hate speaker who prefers to perform his hate speech to large audiences in person — where his charisma can shine — but who also knows full well that in order to be convicted of stirring up religious hatred offences in England and Wales, say, public prosecutors must prove both intent to stir up hatred and the use of threatening words or behaviour. Such a hate speaker has reason to be ingenious in how he or she goes about performing acts of hate speech in order to stay one step ahead of the authorities, whether he or she engages in online or offline hate speech.[110]

It is also notable that whilst the nature of online hate is gaining increasing recognition, the issue of online hate directed at women generally remains at the boundaries of these developments.[111]

4.5 Online misogyny as a hate crime

As discussed in the preceding chapters, the widespread nature of online misogyny and its serious impact on the victims stands in stark contrast to the lack of legal responses to that problem. Although misogyny does not fall within the purview of hate crime legislation in England & Wales, and in Scotland, the past couple of years have witnessed an increase in various public and policy initiatives raising awareness of online and offline misogyny. From victims of online

110 Alexander Brown, 'What is so Special About Online (as Compared to Offline) Hate Speech?' (2018) 18 Ethnicities 297, 309.

111 For instance, as of September 2018, the Law Commission consultation on "offensive online communications" launched in February 2018 has not yet considered online gender-based hate in the context of offensive online communications. See Law Commission 'Offensive Online Communications: Current Project Status' (*Law Commission*, 5 February 2018) <www.lawcom.gov.uk/project/offensive-online-communications/> accessed 10 September 2018.

misogyny publicly speaking out, to proposed policy changes and political debates, the issue of online misogyny has gradually attracted the interest of the public.[112] For instance, the Nottinghamshire Police started to flag misogyny as a hate crime in 2016. Although the position on recording misogyny hate crime nationally is not yet clear, a similar approach has been adopted by the police in other regions of England.[113] Between April 2016 and March 2018, 174 women have reported misogyny hate crimes to Nottinghamshire Police[114] and, of these, 73 have been classified as crimes and 101 have been classified as incidents.[115] Importantly, 95.3% of respondents thought that the behaviours distinguished by the Nottinghamshire Police as misogyny hate crime were a social issue which is a particular problem for women (90.4%).[116] However, although behaviours distinguished by the Nottinghamshire Police involved instances of online abuse,[117] there is no specific data on how many of the reported instances of misogyny hate crimes involved online misogyny.

Progressively, a view is shared that the law – and hate crime legislation specifically – ought to respond to instances of online and offline misogyny. In March 2018, the House of Commons debate on misogyny as a hate crime was held, expressing support for a change of law in this

112 Caroline Criado-Perez, 'Caroline Criado-Perez's Speech on Cyber-Harassment at the Women's Aid Conference', *The New Statesman* (London, 4 September 2013) <www.newstatesman.com/internet/2013/09/caroline-criado-perezs-speech-cyber-harassment-womens-aid-conference> accessed 10 September 2018; Emma A Jane, *Misogyny Online: A Short (and Brutish) History* (SAGE 2017); Barker and Jurasz, 'Submission of Evidence on Online Violence Against Women to the UN Special Rapporteur on Violence Against Women' (n 95); Barker and Jurasz, *Submission of Evidence to Scottish Government Independent Review of Hate Crime Legislation (Bracadale Review)* (n 12).

113 Home Affairs Committee, *Hate Crime: Abuse, Hate and Extremism Online* (HC 2016–17, 609) Q383. As of 5 September 2018, only select police forces in England record misogyny hate crime and gender hate crime. No equivalent initiative has been taken by the police in Scotland nor Wales. See also the discussions above at 4.3. Extending the boundaries of hate crime: hate (re)defined.

114 Louise Mullany and Loretta Trickett, 'Misogyny Hate Crime Evaluation Report' (*Nottingham Women's Centre*, 9 July 2018) <www.nottinghamwomenscentre.com/wp-content/uploads/2018/07/Misogyny-Hate-Crime-Evaluation-Report-June-2018.pdf> accessed 10 September 2018.

115 ibid.

116 ibid, 5–6.

117 ibid, 5. Behaviours included: whistling, leering, groping, sexual assault, being followed home, taking unwanted photos on mobiles, upskirting, sexually explicit language, threatening/aggressive/intimidating behaviour, indecent exposure, unwanted sexual advances and online abuse.

direction.[118] Informed by the recent reports of the increase in online abuse faced by female politicians, although not limited to that issue, the debate suggested that categorisation of misogyny as a hate crime is overdue. Furthermore, the significance of recognition of misogyny as a hate crime was aptly captured by Labour MP Stella Creasy:

> What is so powerful about recognising misogyny as a hate crime is identifying that that is not normal human behaviour. It is not about men and women flirting with each other; it is not about men and women being able to banter with each other; it is not about men and women being able to ask each other out. (. . .) It is about being able to say that this sort of behaviour is holding too many back in our society.[119]

Creasy's commitment to fighting misogyny has also been reflected in the result of the vote to amend the Voyeurism (Offences) Bill in September 2018, which opened the way to review of hate crime laws and, possibly, making misogyny a hate crime.[120] But what is needed to make online misogyny a hate crime? Unsurprisingly, there are various approaches to this issue, representing not only diverse viewpoints, but also varying degrees of appreciation of the difficulties posed by the complicated and overly fragmented legal landscape.[121]

The view advocated for here is that two key steps ought to be taken in order for the law to enable the punishment of online misogyny as a hate crime. First, gender needs to be added to a list of protected characteristics under hate crime legislation in England & Wales[122] and second, the law requires reform to address offences committed on or using social media.

The first element is significant in that it will enable the prosecution of offences motivated by gender-based hostility, prejudice or bias, thereby sending the message that such behaviours are socially unacceptable and will be punished by law. Such addition would also make hate crime legislation more aligned with equality legislation

118 House of Commons Library, *Debate Pack: Misogyny as a Hate Crime* (compiled by Sarah Pepin, CDP-2018-0057, 6 March 2018); HC Deb 7 March 2018, vol 637, cols 132–49.

119 HC Deb 7 March 2018, vol 637, col 136.

120 Brooks, 'Review Brings Misogyny as a Hate Crime a Step Closer' (n 65).

121 For discussions of the legislative provisions, see generally Chapter 3.

122 As argued above, in section *4.3.2. Gender as a protected characteristic: towards law reform.*

and requisite non-discrimination provisions of international treaties such as CEDAW 1979, which create legally binding obligations on the United Kingdom. However, it is the second element (the creation of a new, underlying offence) that makes it fully enforceable. As was demonstrated in Chapter 3, the current legal provisions concerning online communications, as well as those that could technically apply to instances of online hate, do not work. In addition, the current system is too fragmented, inconsistent and, in some cases, outdated to the extent that any attempts to retro-fit these provisions to prosecute instances of online, gender-based hate compounds the problem rather than remedies it.

Finally, the symbolic impact of creating such offences should not be underestimated. Whilst law reform alone would not suppress misogyny or other forms of gender-based discrimination, it is likely to have an impact on the way in which gender-based harms are perceived within the legal system and accordingly legislated for. Importantly, these two key amendments to legislation would open the possibility of punishing instances of online misogyny and therefore declaring that gender-based hate does not have a place, nor will it be tolerated, on the Internet. Phillipson and Walters' reflection holds true for online misogyny: "legislative restraints on hate speech may not be effective in suppressing it, but may still have a valuable function in declaring that the attitudes in question must never be allowed to become respectable" and whilst "material of this kind exists on the Internet on a large scale, (…) there is a social consensus that it must never find its way into respectable political or academic discourse."[123]

4.6 Conclusions

Misogynistic social media abuse is not only a form of online hate speech but frequently amounts to incitement of hatred towards women as well as to the commission of acts of violence against a particular woman (or women in general). Nonetheless, the law has been slow in responding to this problem and its broader impact. The law in England & Wales (and, until recently, in Scotland) has also appeared reluctant to add gender as a protected characteristic in the context of hate crime, despite the existence of similar provisions under equality legislation.[124]

123 Law Commission, *Hate Crime: Should the Current Offences be Extended?* (n 44) 189.
124 Equality Act 2010, s 4.

Bibliography

Table of cases

Delfi AS v Estonia App no 64569/09 (ECtHR, 16 June 2015)
Erbakan v Turkey App no 59405/00 (ECtHR, 6 July 2006)
Handyside v UK App no 5493/72 (ECtHR, 7 December 1976)
Vejdeland v Sweden App no 1813/07 (ECtHR, 9 February 2012)

Table of legislation and international treaties

UK Public General Acts
Crime and Disorder Act 1998
Criminal Justice Act 2003
Equal Pay Act 1970
Equality Act 2010
Public Order Act 1986
Race Relations Act 1965
Representation of People Act 1918

Acts of the Scottish Parliament
Criminal Justice (Scotland) Act 2003 (asp 7)

US Statutes
Equal Pay Act of 1963, 29 USC § 206(d)

International Treaties
Convention on the Elimination of All Forms of Discrimination Against Women (adopted 18 December 1979, entered into force 3 September 1981) 1249 UNTS 13 (CEDAW)
Convention on the Prevention and Punishment of the Crime of Genocide (adopted 9 December 1948, entered into force 12 January 1951) 1021 UNTS 278 (Genocide Convention)
International Convention on the Elimination of All Forms of Racial Discrimination (opened for signature 21 December 1965, entered into force 4 January 1969) 660 UNTS 212 (ICERD)
International Covenant on Civil and Political Rights (adopted 16 December 1966, entered into force 23 March 1976) 999 UNTS 171 (ICCPR)

Table of Bills
Voyeurism (Offences) Bill 2018

List of secondary sources

Books
Chakraborti N and Garland J, *Hate Crime: Impact, Causes & Responses* (2nd edn, SAGE 2015)
Citron DK, *Hate Crimes in Cyberspace* (Harvard University Press 2014)

Conaghan J, *Law and Gender* (OUP, 2013)

Daniels J, *Cyber Racism: White Supremacy Online and the New Attack on Civil Rights* (Rowman & Littlefield Publishers 2009)

Hall N, *Hate Crime* (2nd edn, Routledge 2013)

Iganski P, *'Hate Crime' and the City* (The Policy Press 2008)

Jane EA, *Misogyny Online: A Short (and Brutish) History* (SAGE 2017)

Jenness V and Grattet R, *Making Hate A Crime: From Social Movement to Law Enforcement* (Russell Sage Foundation 2001)

Lawrence FM, *Punishing Hate: Bias Crimes under American Law* (Harvard University Press 1999)

Perry B, *In the Name of Hate: Understanding Hate Crimes* (Routledge 2001)

Poland B, *Haters: Harassment, Abuse, and Violence Online* (University of Nebraska Press 2016)

Waldron J, *The Harm in Hate Speech* (Harvard University Press 2012)

Williams M, *Virtually Criminal: Crime, Deviance and Regulation Online* (Routledge 2006)

Conference Papers

Barker K and Jurasz O, 'Online Misogyny as Hate Crime: Tweeting Sense, Slaying Trolls' (Society of Legal Scholars Conference, Dublin, September 2017)

Contributions to Edited Books

Bakalis C, 'Regulating Hate Crime in the Digital Age' in Schweppe J and Walters MA (eds), *The Globalization of Hate: Internationalizing Hate Crime?* (OUP 2016)

Bleich E, 'From Race to Hate: *A Historical Perspective*' in Brudholm T and Johansen BS (eds), *Hate, Politics, Law: Critical Perspectives on Combatting Hate* (OUP 2018)

Chakraborti N and Garland J, 'Hate Crime' in DeKeseredy WS and Dragiewicz M (eds), *Routledge Handbook of Critical Criminology* (Routledge 2011)

Douglas KM, 'Psychology, Discrimination and Hate Groups Online' in Joinson A and others (eds), *The Oxford Handbook of Internet Psychology* (OUP 2007)

Mason-Bish H, 'Beyond the Silo: Rethinking Hate Crime and Intersectionality' in Hall N and others (eds), *The Routledge International Handbook on Hate Crime* (Routledge 2014)

Perry B, 'The Sociology of Hate: Theoretical Approaches' in Levin B (ed), *Hate Crimes: Understanding and Defining Hate Crime* (Praeger Publications, 2009)

Council of Europe Publications and Resolutions

Council of Europe, *Council of Europe Gender Equality Strategy 2014–2017* (Council of Europe, February 2014) <https://rm.coe.int/1680590174> accessed 10 September 2018

Council of Europe, *Council of Europe Gender Equality Strategy 2018–2023* (Council of Europe, June 2018) <https://rm.coe.int/prems-093618-gbr-gender-equality-strategy-2023-web-a5/16808b47e1> accessed 10 September 2018

Council of Europe, 'Ending Cyberdiscrimination and Online Hate' (CoE Res 2144, text adopted 25 January 2017)

Council of Europe, 'Putting an End to Sexual Violence and Harassment of Women in Public Space' (CoE Res 2177, text adopted 29 June 2017)

Council of Europe Parliamentary Assembly Committee on Equality and Non-Discrimination, 'Ending Cyberdiscrimination and Online Hate, Report by Rapporteur Marit Maij' (13 December 2016) Doc 14217 <http://semantic-pace.net/tools/pdf.aspx?doc=aHR0cDovL2Fzc2VtYmx5LmNvZS5pbnQvbncveG1sL1hSZWYvWDJILURXLWV4dHIuYXNwP2ZpbGVpZD0yMzIzNCZsYW5nPUVO&xsl=aHR0cDovL3NlbWFudGljcGFjZS5uZXQvWHNsdC9QZGYvWFJlZi1XRC1BVC1YTUwyUERGLnhzbA==&xsltparams=ZmlsZWlkPTIzMjM0> accessed 10 September 2018

Evidence Submissions

Barker K and Jurasz O, 'Submission of Evidence on Online Violence Against Women to the UN Special Rapporteur on Violence Against Women, its Causes and Consequences, Dr Dubravka Šimonović' (*Open University*, November 2017) <http://oro.open.ac.uk/52611/> accessed 10 September 2018

Barker K and Jurasz O, 'Submission of Evidence to Scottish Government Independent Review of Hate Crime Legislation (Bracadale Review)' (*Open University*, December 2017) <http://oro.open.ac.uk/52612/> accessed 10 September 2018

Governmental Publications

Cabinet Office, *Protecting the Debate: Intimidation, Influence and Information* (HM Government, 29 July 2018) <https://assets.publishing.service.gov.uk/government/uploads/system/uploads/attachment_data/file/730209/CSPL.pdf> accessed 10 September 2018

O'Neill A, *Hate Crime, England and Wales, 2016/17* (Home Office, Statistical Bulletin 17/7, 10 October 2017)

Scottish Government, *Delivering for Today, Investing for Tomorrow: The Government's Programme for Scotland 2018 – 19* (Scottish Government, September 2018) <www.gov.scot/Resource/0053/00539972.pdf> accessed 10 September 2018

Scottish Government, *Independent Review of Hate Crime Legislation in Scotland: Consultation Paper* (Scottish Government, August 2017) <www.gov.scot/Resource/0052/00524055.pdf> accessed 10 September 2018 (Bracadale Review)

Scottish Government, *Independent Review of Hate Crime Legislation in Scotland: Final Report* (Scottish Government, May 2018) <www.gov.scot/Resource/0053/00535892.pdf> accessed 10 September 2018 (Bracadale Review: Final Report)

Hansard Reports

HC Deb 12 July 2017, vol 627, cols 159–160

HC Deb 7 March 2018, vol 637, cols 132–149

IGO Documents and Publications

European Commission against Racism and Intolerance, ECRI General Policy Recommendation No 15 on Combating Hate Speech (Council of Europe, adopted 8 December 2015) <https://rm.coe.int/ecri-general-policy-recommendation-no-15-on-combating-hate-speech/16808b5b01> accessed 10 September 2018

Gagliardone I and others, *Countering Online Hate Speech* (UNESCO 2015) <http://unesdoc.unesco.org/images/0023/002332/233231e.pdf> accessed 10 September 2018

OSCE, *Hate Crime Laws: A Practical Guide* (OSCE Office for Democratic Institutions and Human Rights (ODIHR) 2009) <www.osce.org/odihr/36426?download=true> accessed 10 September 2018

Journal Articles

Alkiviadou N, 'Regulating Internet Hate: A Flying Pig?' (2016) 7 JIPITEC 216

———, 'Hate Speech on Social Media Networks: Towards a Regulatory Framework?' (2018) I& CTL (published online 4 July 2018) <https://doi.org/10.1080/13600834.2018.1494417> accessed 10 September 2018.

Angelari M, 'Hate Crime Statutes: A Promising Tool for Fighting Violence Against Women' (1994) 2 AmUJGender & L 63

Bakalis C, 'The Victims of Hate Crime and the Principles of the Criminal Law' (2017) 37 LS 718

Banks J, 'Regulating Hate Speech Online' (2010) 24(3) IRLCT 233

Brown A, 'The 'Who' Question in the Hate Speech Debate: Part 1: Consistency, Practical, and Formal Approaches' (2016) 29 CJLJ 275

———, 'What is so Special About Online (as Compared to Offline) Hate Speech?' (2018) 18 Ethnicities 297

Brown C, 'Legislating Against Hate Crime in New Zealand: The Need to Recognise Gender-Based Violence' (2004) 35 VUWLR 591

Choundas GP, 'Neither Equal nor Protected: The Invisible Law of Equal Protection, the Legal Invisibility of its Gender-Based Victims' (1995) 44 Emory LJ 1069

Garland J and Chakraborti N, 'Divided by a Common Concept: Assessing the Implications of Different Conceptualisations of Hate Crime in the European Union' (2012) 9 EJC 38

Gerstenfeld PB, Grant DR and Chiang C-P, 'Hate Online: A Content Analysis of Extremist Internet Sites' (2003) 3 ASAP 29

Maher JM, McCulloch J and Mason G, 'Punishing Gendered Violence as Hate Crime: Aggravated Sentences as a Means of Recognising Hate as Motivation for Violent Crimes Against Women' (2015) 41 AFLJ 177

Mason G, 'Victim Attributes in Hate Crime Law: Difference and Politics of Justice' (2014) 54 BritJCriminol 161

Mason-Bish H and Gill AK, 'Addressing Violence Against Women as a Form of Hate Crime: Limitations and Possibilities' (2013) 105 Feminist Review 1

Moran LJ and Sharpe AN, 'Violence, Identity and Policing: The Case of Violence Against Transgender People' (2004) 4 Criminal Justice 395

Reidy DA, 'Hate Crimes, Oppression and Legal Theory' (2002) 16 Public Affairs Quarterly 259

Schweppe J, 'Defining Characteristics and Politicizing Victims: A Legal Perspective' (2012) 10 Journal of Hate Studies 173

Walters MA and Tumath J, 'Gender 'Hostility', Rape, and the Hate Crime Paradigm' (2014) 77 MLR 563

Weisburd SB and Levin B, 'On the Basis of Sex: Recognizing Gender-Based Bias Crimes' (1994) 5 Stan L & Pol'y Rev 21

Weston-Scheuber K, 'Gender and the Prohibition of Hate Speech' (2012) 12 QUT Law & Justice Journal 132

Law Commission Reports

Law Commission, *Hate Crime: The Case for Extending the Existing Offences* (Law Com CP No 213, 2013)

Law Commission, *Hate Crime: Should the Current Offences be Extended?* (Law Com No 348, 2014)

Newspaper Articles

Ashcroft E, 'Cat-Calling and Wolf-Whistling Now Classed as Gender-Hate Crimes by Avon and Somerset Police' *Bristol Post* (Bristol, 16 October 2017) <www.bristolpost.co.uk/news/bristol-news/gender-hate-now-recognised-crime-635194?utm_content=bufferf8757&utm_medium=social&utm_source=twitter.com&utm_campaign=buffer> accessed 10 September 2018.

Boothman J, 'Academics Tell Bracadale Review: Make Online Misogynistic Abuse a Hate Crime' *The Times* (London, 8 April 2018) <www.thetimes.co.uk/article/academics-tell-bracadale-review-make-online-misogynistic-abuse-a-hate-crime-lfqcx2jt7> accessed 10 September 2018

Brooks L, 'Review Brings Misogyny as a Hate Crime a Step Closer' *The Guardian* (London, 6 September 2018) <www.theguardian.com/society/2018/sep/05/first-step-to-misogyny-becoming-a-hate-called-amazing-victory> accessed 10 September 2018

Criado-Perez C, 'Caroline Criado-Perez's Speech on Cyber-Harassment at the Women's Aid Conference', *The New Statesman* (London, 4 September 2013) <www.newstatesman.com/internet/2013/09/caroline-criado-perezs-speech-cyber-harassment-womens-aid-conference> accessed 10 September 2018

Dodd V, 'CPS to Crack Down on Social Media Hate Crime, Says Alison Saunders' *The Guardian* (London, 21 August 2017) <www.theguardian.com/society/2017/aug/21/cps-to-crack-down-on-social-media-hate-says-alison-saunders> accessed 10 September 2018

Lee D, Elliott F and Gibb F, 'MPs to Vote on Making Misogyny a Hate Crime in Legal First' *The Times* (London, 4 September 2018) <www.thetimes.co.uk/article/mps-to-vote-on-making-misogyny-a-hate-crime-in-legal-first-3qpwl766p> accessed 10 September 2018

Saunders A, 'Hate is Hate. Online Abusers Must Be Dealt with Harshly' *The Guardian* (London, 21 August 2017) <www.theguardian.com/commentisfree/2017/aug/20/hate-crimes-online-abusers-prosecutors-serious-crackdown-

internet-face-to-face?utm_source=dlvr.it&utm_medium=twitter> accessed 10 September 2018

Sylvester R and Thomson A, 'Diane Abbott Interview: 'Why Am I Abused So Much? I'm Both Black and a Woman'' *The Times* (London, 28 April 2018) <www.thetimes.co.uk/article/diane-abbott-saturday-interview-why-am-i-abused-so-much-i-m-both-black-and-a-woman-fd2vhdrc5> accessed 10 September 2018

Townsend M, 'Police in England and Wales Consider Making Misogyny a Hate Crime' *The Guardian* (London, 10 September 2016) <www.theguardian.com/society/2016/sep/10/misogyny-hate-crime-nottingham-police-crackdown> accessed 10 September 2018

Parliamentary Publications and Reports

Home Affairs Committee, *Hate Crime: Abuse, Hate and Extremism Online* (HC 2016–17, 609)

House of Commons Library, *Debate Pack: Misogyny as a Hate Crime* (compiled by Sarah Pepin, CDP-2018–0057, 6 March 2018)

Publications of Professional Bodies

College of Policing, *Hate Crime Operational Guidance* (College of Policing, May 2014) <www.college.police.uk/What-we-do/Support/Equality/Documents/Hate-Crime-Operational-Guidance.pdf> accessed 10 September 2018

Reports

Chalmers J and Leverick F, *A Comparative Analysis of Hate Crime Legislation: A Report to the Hate Crime Legislation Review* (Scottish Government, July 2017) <https://consult.gov.scot/hate-crime/independent-review-of-hate-crime-legislation/supporting_documents/495517_APPENDIX%20%20ACADEMIC%20REPORT.pdf> accessed 10 September 2018

Mullany L and Trickett L, 'Misogyny Hate Crime Evaluation Report' (*Nottingham Women's Centre*, 9 July 2018) <www.nottinghamwomenscentre.com/wp-content/uploads/2018/07/Misogyny-Hate-Crime-Evaluation-Report-June-2018.pdf> accessed 10 September 2018

Walters MA, Brown R and Wiedlitzka S, *Research Report 102: Causes and Motivations of Hate Crime* (Equality and Human Rights Commission, July 2016) <www.equalityhumanrights.com/sites/default/files/research-report-102-causes-and-motivations-of-hate-crime.pdf> accessed 10 September 2018

Websites

Amnesty International, 'Toxic Twitter – A Toxic Place for Women' (*Amnesty International*, 2018) <www.amnesty.org/en/latest/research/2018/03/online-violence-against-women-chapter-1/> accessed 10 September 2018

APPG, 'Inquiries' (*APPG Hate Crime*, 2018) <www.appghatecrime.org/inquiries/> accessed 10 September 2018

CPS, 'Hate Crime' (*Crown Prosecution Service*, 2017) <www.cps.gov.uk/hate-crime> accessed 10 September 2018

Dhrodia A, 'Unsocial Media: Tracking Twitter Abuse against Women MPs' (*Medium*, 3 September 2017) <https://medium.com/@AmnestyInsights/

unsocial-media-tracking-twitter-abuse-against-women-mps-fc28aeca498a> accessed 10 September 2018

Facebook, 'Community Standards' (*Facebook*, 2018) <www.facebook.com/communitystandards/hate_speech> accessed 10 September 2018

Home Office, 'Home Secretary Announces New National Online Hate Crime Hub' (*HM Government*, 8 October 2017) <www.gov.uk/government/news/home-secretary-announces-new-national-online-hate-crime-hub> accessed 10 September 2018

Law Commission 'Offensive Online Communications: Current Project Status' (*Law Commission*, 5 February 2018) <www.lawcom.gov.uk/project/offensive-online-communications/> accessed 10 September 2018

Mayor of London, 'Mayor Launches New Unit to Tackle Online Hate Crime' (*Mayor of London and London Assembly*, 24 April 2017) <www.london.gov.uk/press-releases/mayoral/mayor-launches-unit-to-tackle-online-hate-crime> accessed 10 September 2018

North Yorkshire Police, 'Misogyny to be Recognised as a Hate Crime from Wednesday 10 May 2017' (*North Yorkshire Police*, 10 May 2017) <https://northyorkshire.police.uk/news/misogyny-recognised-hate-crime-wednesday-10-may-2017/> accessed 10 September 2018

Nottinghamshire Police, 'Hate Crime' (*Nottinghamshire Police*, 2018) <www.nottinghamshire.police.uk/hatecrime> accessed 10 September 2018

ORG, 'ORG Response to CPS Announcement on Social Media Hate Crime' (*Open Rights Group*, 21 August 2017) <www.openrightsgroup.org/press/releases/2017/org-response-to-cps-announcement-on-social-media-hate-crime> accessed 10 September 2018

Twitter, 'Twitter Terms of Service' (*Twitter*, effective 25 May 2018) <https://twitter.com/en/tos#intlTerms> accessed 10 September 2018

Voorhoof D, 'Qualification of News Portal as Publisher of Users' Comment May Have Far-Reaching Consequences for Online Freedom of Expression: Delfi AS v. Estonia' (*Strasbourg Observers*, 25 October 2013) <https://strasbourgobservers.com/2013/10/25/qualification-of-news-portal-as-publisher-of-users-comment-may-have-far-reaching-consequences-for-online-freedom-of-expression-delfi-as-v-estonia/> accessed 10 September 2018

5 OVAW and hate

Unfinished (legal) business

> [W]hat is the reason behind this phenomenon? The social construction of online violence is flawed, as is the absence of appropriate regulation and enforcement. This is largely due to the social construction we adopt for the regulation of digital spaces. There is a conception that our "online" is very different from our "offline," yet, even if this is the situation, the standard concepts that have been adopted are now in need of some pressing reconstruction.[1]

5.1 The realities of everyday, gender-based hate

The (mis)perception that gender-based hate, both offline and online, is something incidental and particular to some women only (e.g. female politicians), rather than occurring every day, on a large scale, and happening to women from a variety of demographics, is commonplace. Similar to other forms of violence against women, gender-based hate has become 'normalised' and, due to the lack of social and legal condemnation of it (e.g. in the form of punishment as a hate crime), it slips under the radar of 'legal regulation'. Gendered hate instances have to reach a threshold which is shocking or tragic (such as the murder of Labour politician Jo Cox in June 2016) or must amount to breathtakingly high numbers in order to even register on the scale of what warrants public, social or legal concern.

This in turn has implications for the victims of intersectional hate crime and the victims of gender-based hate alike. For the first category of victims, where gender intersects with one of the protected

1 Kim Barker and Olga Jurasz, 'Gender, Human Rights and Cybercrime: Are Virtual Worlds Really That Different?' in Michael Asimow, Kathryn Brown and David Ray Papke (eds), *Law and Popular Culture: International Perspectives* (Cambridge Scholars Publishing 2014) 87.

DOI: 10.4324/9780429956805-5

characteristics (e.g. religion or disability), the gender aspect of hostility, prejudice or bias is rendered invisible in the eyes of the law and the criminal justice system. Whilst a successful prosecution of a committed offence as a hate crime is likely to succeed (due to the existence of 'hostility, prejudice or bias' based on a protected characteristic being one of the motivating factors), the message sent through such an approach is that gender hostility, gender prejudice or gender bias, are less worthy of protection than other characteristics and gendered forms of hostility will go unpunished – even where they result in acts of violence. The same applies to the second category of victims, for whom the picture is entirely bleak. The gendered nature of their hate victimisation is not only rendered invisible, but there exist no prospects of prosecuting the offence committed against them as a hate crime. This is a significant failing of the current legal system which is yet to be redressed. It is however, not the only failing. Society is also – at least partially – responsible, and the endemic nature of gendered hostility is so deeply embedded that even acknowledging that *there is* an issue is a significant obstacle to overcome.

5.2 Online misogyny: not a legislative priority

Law certainly has a central role to play in addressing online misogyny. However, as noted in Chapter 1, the continual gender-bias of the law – spanning its substantive provisions, procedural aspects, and legal actors – poses limitations to the transformative effects of any legal reform in this area. The deeply embedded socio-cultural nature of misogyny means that it is practically impossible to foresee a situation whereby the typically male-dominated judicial bodies, policing institutions, and crime prevention agencies are in a position to challenge the existing – and accepted – norms. Moreover, any efforts to regulate gender-based hate online would require a thorough understanding of the impact of such harms on individuals (across both online and offline spheres) – an understanding clearly articulated in the sentencing remarks of Riddle J in *R v Nimmo & Sorley*,[2] yet completely overlooked and ultimately dismissed as a legislative priority by the House of Lords in 2015.[3]

2 *R v Nimmo and Sorley* (Westminster Magistrates' Court, 24 January 2014).

3 Communications Select Committee, *Social Media and Criminal Offences* (HL 2014–15, 37), para 32.

This dismissal – whilst rationalised in the House of Lords report – is alarmingly negligent and has proved to be incredibly short-sighted given the prevalence of online text-based abuses and, especially, the increasing numbers of women and girls reporting online harassment. The sole chance to rectify this oversight came in 2016 with the opportunity to introduce the Malicious Communications (Social Media) Bill[4] – which promised to introduce penalties and sentences for threats made over social media. This – in itself – was not a significant aim but the Bill remains nonetheless an important indicator of the potential willingness, at least by a private member,[5] to raise the issue of social media abuse in the context of law reform.

Given the limitations of the House of Lords, and the Malicious Communications Bill, any agenda for legislative reform in this area has been truly dismissed. It is therefore ultimately unsurprising that few substantive measures have appeared on the statute book, or even in a forum for debate. The lack of action here crosses both parliamentary chambers – it can only be hoped that the Law Commission Project[6] examining social media offences, together with the promised Internet Safety Strategy,[7] combine to offer realistic and meaningful opportunities to tackle online text-based abuses.

Although the House of Lords did not set out to consider gender-based online abuse, its decision not to create offences dealing with social media abuse has a significant ripple effect. This is particularly notable in the context of online hate crimes – due to the absence of such provisions the law displays significant limitations in terms of prosecuting such behaviours, even in situations where they are motivated by prejudice, hatred, or bias based on one of the already protected characteristics.

4 Malicious Communications (Social Media) HC Bill (2016–17) [44].

5 The Malicious Communications (Social Media) Bill (2016) was presented to the House of Commons by Anna Turley MP, and supported by – amongst others – Melanie Onn MP.

6 As of September 2018, the Law Commission consultation on 'offensive online communications', launched in February 2018, has not yet considered online gender-based hate in the context of offensive online communications. Law Commission, 'Offensive Online Communications: Current Project Status' (*Law Commission*, 5 February 2018) <www.lawcom.gov.uk/project/offensive-online-communications/> accessed 10 September 2018.

7 Department for Digital, Culture, Media & Sport, *Internet Safety Strategy* (Green Paper, 2017).

5.3 Implications for legal response and regulation

In principle, the online nature of hate should not be a barrier to prosecuting hate crimes. Although the environment in which hate occurs is different, the seriousness of the impact on the recipient of the hateful act/message should not be downplayed. In fact, the anonymity, volume, and public nature of such hateful acts (just to name a few factors) arguably exacerbate the impact on, and harm caused to the victim.[8] However, online hate speech poses certain challenges to the ways in which law can respond. Therefore, any comprehensive legal response needs to take account of two concurrent factors characterising online misogyny – its gender-based nature and online manifestations.

This book explores the current legal framework dealing with communication offences, demonstrating that whilst some of them *can* in principle be used to establish accountability for some acts of online hate, they nonetheless fall short of having an adequate focus to address instances of online misogyny – especially when it takes the form of online text-based abuse.[9] In particular, it has highlighted that the law's main deficiencies are embedded in its exclusive focus on online image-based abuses as well as misuses of public communications networks, which result in what has ultimately become the failure of the legislative regulatory framework to address online misogyny. Furthermore, whilst a number of offences can be 'retro-fitted'[10] in an attempt to address the modern phenomena of online hate and online misogyny, these, together with their respective thresholds and tests, result in a contradictory and unnecessarily complex legal landscape which effectively prevents any adequate responses.

Where new offences dealing with selected aspects of online abuse have been introduced, the law focuses exclusively on the image-based nature of such abuses most recently culminating in the vote on amending the Voyeurism Bill to include new, standalone offences of upskirting.[11] Although the vote also resulted in the announcement of

8 For a discussion of harms and the impact on the victims, see Chapter 2.

9 See generally discussions of legislative provisions for communications misuse in Chapter 3.

10 See Chapter 3, 3.4. Threats and threats to kill.

11 In particular, the second version of the Voyeurism (Offences) Bill proposed introduction of 'two new offences into the Sexual Offences Act 2003 for instances where, without consent, a person operates equipment or records an image under another person's clothing with the intention of viewing, or enabling another person to view, their genitals or buttocks, with or without underwear. The offences would apply where the offender had a motive of either a) obtaining sexual gratification, or b)

the Government's commitment to a review of hate crime laws (with particular consideration given to making misogyny a hate crime) these developments present few causes for celebration. Despite a significant amount of campaigning (especially by Stella Creasy, Melanie Onn, and Lucy Powell, to name but three prominent women) to make misogyny a hate crime, also backed up by a noteworthy media presence and the support of some of the key third sector organisations (e.g. The Fawcett Society),[12] the steps taken so far have grossly ignored tackling misogyny in the online realm. Instead, the true focus of these campaigns appears to be aligned with law's already demonstrated preference for addressing the matters of 'offline' misogyny embodied in the street harassment of women, wolf whistling, and upskirting.

Furthermore, the third sector interventions supposedly to make misogyny a hate crime have largely focussed on the debate of whether to add gender as a protected characteristic or add misogyny as a protected characteristic,[13] largely ignoring the fact that, in some instances, the preliminary issue to be addressed is one concerning the lack of any appropriate legal provisions dealing with online abuse – especially that perpetrated via social media. Whilst the widespread

---

causing humiliation, distress or alarm to the victim. The bill would also ensure that the most serious sexual offenders (where the purpose of the offending is for sexual gratification) are made subject to notification requirements.' Ministry of Justice, *Voyeurism (Offences) (No. 2) Bill Factsheet* (HM Government Policy Document, 21 June 2018) <https://assets.publishing.service.gov.uk/government/uploads/system/uploads/attachment_data/file/718308/voyeurism-offences-bill-factsheet.pdf> accessed 10 September 2018.

12 Fawcett Society, 'Fawcett Supports Stella Creasy's Amendment to Recognize Misogyny as a Hate Crime' (*Fawcett Society*, 5 September 2018) <www.fawcettsociety.org.uk/news/fawcett-supports-stella-creasys-proposed-amendment-to-recognize-misogyny-as-a-hate-crime> accessed 10 September 2018.

13 For instance, the Fawcett Society advocated for including misogyny as a category for enhanced sentencing purposes and, potentially, as an aggravated offence. In contrast, the Final Report of the Bracadale Review suggested that gender ought to be added as a protected characteristic within hate crime legislation in Scotland, but ultimately rejected explicit inclusion of misogyny within the new hate crime provisions, including creation of a standalone offence of misogynistic harassment. ENGENDER, *Engender Submission to the Independent Review of Hate Crime Legislation in Scotland* (ENGENDER, November 2017) 21 <www.engender.org.uk/content/publications/Engender-submission-to-the-Independent-Review-of-Hate-Crime-Legislation-in-Scotland.pdf> accessed 10 September 2018; Fawcett Society, *Sex Discrimination Law Review* (Fawcett Society, January 2018) 15 <www.fawcettsociety.org.uk/Handlers/Download.ashx?IDMF=e473a103-28c1-4a6c-aa43-5099d34c0116> accessed 10 September 2018.

nature of online, gender-based hate and OVAW is occasionally noted in these interventions and campaigns, online misogyny perpetrated via online text-based abuse has thus far been ignored. As such, these efforts, although notable and important from other perspectives, still fall short of comprehensive responses to the gender-based social issue of online abuse. Such campaigns – whilst glossy and publicity oriented – often lack substance and, accordingly, continue to perpetuate the failings in this area. They are therefore – possibly – well-intentioned, but sadly lacking in results.

5.4 Final thought

The substantive provisions which could be retro-fitted to potentially address online text-based abuses all have significantly high thresholds for prosecution – as such, it is therefore time for a refreshed, alternative approach which criminalises disruptive behaviour online. Such a shift could allow a new offence – or offences – to operate at a much lower threshold – but one which remains sufficiently high to capture *only* criminal conduct – and which could offer means of redress to victims.

More broadly, as advocated for in this volume, two-stage law reform is needed in order to adequately address, punish, and combat misogynistic online abuse, first by adding gender as a protected characteristic under hate crime legislation in England & Wales and second, by creating new offences committed on or using social media – including that of disruptive behaviour online. A failure to implement such reforms is a failure to treat issues of online, gender-based hate seriously. It is also a monumental failure of the law in securing *de facto* equality.

Bibliography

Table of cases

R v Nimmo & Sorley (Westminster Magistrates' Court, 24 January 2014)

Table of Bills

Malicious Communications (Social Media) HC Bill (2016–17) [44]

List of secondary sources

Command Papers

Department for Digital, Culture, Media & Sport, *Internet Safety Strategy* (Green Paper, 2017)

Consultation Responses

ENGENDER, *Engender Submission to the Independent Review of Hate Crime Legislation in Scotland* (ENGENDER, November 2017) <www.engender.org.uk/content/publications/Engender-submission-to-the-Independent-Review-of-Hate-Crime-Legislation-in-Scotland.pdf> accessed 10 September 2018

Contributions to Edited Books

Barker K and Jurasz O, 'Gender, Human Rights and Cybercrime: Are Virtual Worlds Really That Different?' in Asimow M, Brown K and Papke DR (eds), *Law and Popular Culture: International Perspectives* (Cambridge Scholars Publishing 2014)

HM Government Policy Documents

Ministry of Justice, *Voyeurism (Offences) (No. 2) Bill Factsheet* (HM Government Policy Document, 21 June 2018) <https://assets.publishing.service.gov.uk/government/uploads/system/uploads/attachment_data/file/718308/voyeurism-offences-bill-factsheet.pdf> accessed 10 September 2018

NGO Reports

Fawcett Society, *Sex Discrimination Law Review* (Fawcett Society, January 2018) <www.fawcettsociety.org.uk/Handlers/Download.ashx?IDMF=e473a103-28c1-4a6c-aa43-5099d34c0116> accessed 10 September 2018

Parliamentary Reports

Communications Select Committee, *Social Media and Criminal Offences* (HL 2014–15, 37)

Websites

Fawcett Society, 'Fawcett Supports Stella Creasy's Amendment to Recognize Misogyny as a Hate Crime' (*Fawcett Society*, 5 September 2018) <www.fawcettsociety.org.uk/news/fawcett-supports-stella-creasys-proposed-amendment-to-recognize-misogyny-as-a-hate-crime> accessed 10 September 2018

Law Commission 'Offensive Online Communications: Current Project Status' (*Law Commission*, 5 February 2018) <www.lawcom.gov.uk/project/offensive-online-communications/> accessed 10 September 2018

Index

Taylor & Francis Group
an informa business

Taylor & Francis eBooks

www.taylorfrancis.com

A single destination for eBooks from Taylor & Francis with increased functionality and an improved user experience to meet the needs of our customers.

90,000+ eBooks of award-winning academic content in Humanities, Social Science, Science, Technology, Engineering, and Medical written by a global network of editors and authors.

TAYLOR & FRANCIS EBOOKS OFFERS:

- A streamlined experience for our library customers
- A single point of discovery for all of our eBook content
- Improved search and discovery of content at both book and chapter level

REQUEST A FREE TRIAL

support@taylorfrancis.com

Routledge
Taylor & Francis Group

CRC Press
Taylor & Francis Group

For Product Safety Concerns and Information please contact our EU representative GPSR@taylorandfrancis.com
Taylor & Francis Verlag GmbH, Kaufingerstraße 24, 80331 München, Germany

www.ingramcontent.com/pod-product-compliance
Ingram Content Group UK Ltd.
Pitfield, Milton Keynes, MK11 3LW, UK
UKHW022157190926
475702UK00003B/70
9781138590373